"our ancient & Loving ffriends"

The Town of Southampton, New York's Relationship with the Shinnecock Indians

1628–1920

James P. Lynch

HERITAGE BOOKS
2009

HERITAGE BOOKS
AN IMPRINT OF HERITAGE BOOKS, INC.

Books, CDs, and more—Worldwide

For our listing of thousands of titles see our website at
www.HeritageBooks.com

Published 2009 by
HERITAGE BOOKS, INC.
Publishing Division
100 Railroad Ave. #104
Westminster, Maryland 21157

Copyright © 2009 James P. Lynch

Other books by the author:

*By "theire free act & deed": Connecticut's
Land Relationship with Indian Tribes, 1496–2003*

*Gideon's Calling: The Founding and Development of the
Schaghticoke Indian Community at Kent, Connecticut, 1638–1854*

All rights reserved. No part of this book may be reproduced or transmitted in any form or by any means, electronic or mechanical, including photocopying, recording or by any information storage and retrieval system without written permission from the author, except for the inclusion of brief quotations in a review.

International Standard Book Numbers
Paperbound: 978-0-7884-5024-2
Clothbound: 978-0-7884-8239-7

For Mike,
astute counselor at law,
mentor, and trusted friend.

Contents

Introduction vii

I. Beginnings 1
   "they enclose noe Land neither have noe habitation"...1
   The Earl's Domain 8
   The "inhabitants of Linne" 10
   "as may be most sutable to theire own comforts" 16

II. The "Seponark Indians" and their Lands 19
   Indian Land Conveyances and Connecticut Law:
      1639-1668 22

III. Settling in 33
   "the above named English shall defend us" 33
   "several insolent injuries & insufferable outrages" 33

IV. The Western Lands 39
   "quiet seizen and possession of all lands" 39
   "all our right, title, and interest" 42
   "the said persons or Indians had noe right" 50

V. "being destitute of such a person" 55

VI. The Thousand Year Lease 61
   "by and with the consent of our people" 61

VII. Transformation 1703-1860 65
   Accommodations 65
   "the wood will soon be done" 68
   "the above Indians shall Improve" 71
   New Ideologies 74
   "towards finishing their Meetinghouse" 76
   "But being feeble": The Canoe Place Chapel 78
   "the tribe had a church": The "Warnertown" Chapel..81

The Church at Shinnecock Neck..82
"we will give them al Shinnecock Neck"......................83

VIII. A New Form of Government..85
"we would aid and Assist them"..85
Racial and Ethnic Tensions..95
"Debarred from Drawing"..97
Land Problems...99
"the white people will not allow us to vote":
The 1822 Petition...101
A Changing Community 104
Controversy..105
The Austin Rose v. Luther Bunn, James Bun, and
Francis Willis suit..106

IX. Resolution 111
A Land of Their Own..113

X. The Western Lands and the Shinnecock 119
More Litigation: The Lands at Canoe Place..............119
"to draw theire lots in Conew place Division":
The Survey and Division of 1738 120
The 1890 Tribal Trustees v. Cassady Suit................128
The 1919 Shinnecock Tribe v. Hubbard Suit...........135

Notes 143

Appendix A. Maps 1-6..157

About the Author..167

Introduction

On June 10, 1640, the sailing ship *Goode Adventure*, out of Boston, entered what is now Peconic Bay on Long Island, sailing along its vast shoreline. One of her passengers, Edward Howell, formerly of the Massachusetts Bay Colony noted, "We sail along the shores of ye Peaconick baye and on the north and on the south wee see a wilderness untouched by ye white man." When *Goode Adventure* anchored in a protected cove she was approached by canoes belonging to the area's Indian inhabitants. As Howell noted, "By looking narrowly we discovered ye chief ones amongst them to come aboard. As it proved one of them was able to speak a few words of Englishe and we made out to understand that we were welcome and might land." As Howell further noted, "Ye Indians offered us venison and maze and made many signs of friendship." Three days later, the new arrivals explored the area finding "a pleasant piece of upland situated between two ponds...we speedily agreede with the Indians to take this for our plantation." Thus, began a relationship that was to be described by the local Indians in terms of "...our ancient & Loving ffriends."

Two events occurred that continue to this present day. First a plantation was established which became the present-day Town of Southampton, New York. Second, a 369-year relationship was established with the natives of the region, one that was of both friendship and conflict.

Historically, Southampton as a town is unique, a political anomaly. Her beginnings were derived from a private land grant. For a period of time Southampton was, like her sister town East Hampton, in of herself, an independent 'mini' colony. Later, the Town sought both the protection of, and political union with, the colony of Connecticut. The

Connecticut General Court of Elections, the colony's legislative body, noting Southampton's distant geographical location, afforded Southampton liberties that were not common to other Connecticut towns. Yet in the end, despite the town's strenuous objections, Southampton was forced into a union with the Province of New York by virtue of a royal grant to the King's brother, James, the Duke of York.

Similarly, the Shinnecock's historical past also had its own uniqueness and analytical perspective. Early in the historic period the local Indians, the Shinnecock, were not politically autonomous. These Indians, at the time of first contact, were known to be politically subordinated to the leadership of the neighboring Montauk tribe. This situation lasted for a period of at least another 22 years (circa 1670), time enough for a person to be born and achieve adulthood knowing no other tribal leadership other than that by a neighboring tribe. Additionally, after 1703 the Shinnecock devolved into a tribal remnant lacking its own land base for a period of 156 years (1703-1859). Within this time period, the Town of Southampton exerted a high degree of legal jurisdiction and political control over this transitioning Indian/African-American/Anglo community.

Like all historical events, the story of the Town and its relations with the Shinnecock did not start with this first arrival of immigrants. The chain of historical events that led to that eventful 1640 meeting upon Peconic Bay began long before that June day. This story began in 1496.

This historical writing focuses principally upon the relationship between what historically became known as the Shinnecock Indians, the government of Great Britain and her colonial policies, the province and later state of New York, and most importantly, the proprietors and residents of the Town of Southampton, Suffolk County, New York.

Previous "revisionist" writings alluding to these events[1] have depicted this relationship in a subjective negative light. They have tended to portray, without direct evidence, this relationship as one of greed, dishonesty, deception, and forced acquisition of the Shinnecock's lands. Unfortunately, the majority of these writings were biased towards a preconceived political agenda, that is, the Indian as victim rather than participant within a historical acculturative progression. One premise of this writing is that the Indian populations of eastern Long Island were not ignorant of the ways of the English settlers. Edward Howell's 1640 observation that the first Indian leader that the new arrivals spoke to was conversant, to a limited degree, in the language of the new arrivals is suggestive that acculturation had preceded their arrival. It will be shown that the political leadership of the Shinnecock had more than average knowledge of English culture, mores, and most importantly, land use and ownership practices at the time of first sustained contact.

A second premise is that the relationship between the Town of Southampton and its Shinnecock neighbors was, on the whole one of peaceful co-existence. This relationship was not without its problems and conflicts, but one continual motif within the historical record was a willingness of the Town leadership to work with, and for, the benefit and well-being of the Shinnecock. Extermination or dispossession based solely on greed was not part of the agenda. Socio-cultural change was. Both the Shinnecock as a community and Southampton as a town changed through time. As a result the nature of the relationship between the two changed also. However, there was always one constant. To this very day the Town has strived to work with, and to reasonably accommodate, the needs and desires of the Shinnecock people.

I. Beginnings

"they enclose noe Land neither have noe settled habitation...."

In the year 1496, King Henry VII of England issued a Royal Patent to the explorer John Cabot. This letter of patent authorized Cabot and his sons to discover and explore "whatsoever isles, countreys, regions or provinces of the heathen and infidels...which before this time have be unknowen to all Christians...."[1] Cabot's charter called for him to "Subdue, Occupy, and Pocess" for the realm any and all lands located in the New World he may encounter during his voyage. The Crown's goal was to acquire dominion, title and jurisdiction over such newly discovered lands.[2]

Cabot's patent or commission followed a pattern of political conquest then known as *Title by Discovery* that emerged from earlier medieval European royal practices. As early as 1109, King Henry I granted one Gilbert de Clare "all the land of Cardigan if he could win it from the Welsh."[3] Similarly, Elisabeth I in her 1584 charter to Sir Walter Raleigh stated that he had liberty to,

> ...discover, search, finde out, and view such remote, heathen and barbarous lands, countries and territories, not actually possessed of any Christian Prince nor inhabited by Christian People..." and to "...have, holde, occupie, and enjoy" the same.[4]

As a result of these and other such patents issued by European monarchs, the concept of *Title by Discovery* or *vacuum domicilium* became an internationally accepted and recognized doctrine under international law. The validity of this concept in American jurisprudence was affirmed by

Supreme Court Justice John Marshall in the Court's 1823 decision in *Johnson and Graham's Lessee v. William M'Intosh.*

This pattern, which the American historian Francis Jennings referred to as "the process of chartered conquest,"[5] consisted of three distinct stages,

> 1. a head of state lay claim to distant territories in jurisdictions other than his own;
>
> 2. he chartered a person or organized groups to conquer the claimed territory in his name but at private expense;
>
> 3. if the conquest was successful, the conquering Lord [whether personal or collective] was recognized by the chartering suzerain as the possessor or governor of the territory, and the hired intern acknowledged the charter's suzerainty or sovereignty. The charter itself served as the new jurisdiction's legal constitution.

The conditions under which such a claim could be made and recognized as valid were,

> The land's occupants were not Christians: The land's occupants did not practice animal husbandry: The land's occupants did not reside in or maintain permanent cities.

At the time of Cabot's 1496 voyage of discovery to New England it was,

> ...accepted as a fundamental law of Christendom that all Christians were in a state of war with all infidels. This was the justification of the permission to 'conquer, occupy, and possess' any non-Christian territories that may be found....[6]

It must be remembered that since circa 637 AD, Christianity had been in a virtual life or death struggle with armies of Islam intent on conquering (*jihad*) and converting Christian Europe. At this time Spain (circa 1498) had recently freed herself from the yoke of Islamic conquest, and the armies of the Islamic Caliphate were laying siege to Vienna.

Islam held a viewpoint similar to Christian Europe concerning non-believers (*kafirs*). As the historian Bernard Lewis noted[7] "it was perfectly legitimate for Muslims to conquer and rule Europe and Europeans and thus enable them...to embrace the true faith. It was a crime and sin for Europeans to conquer and rule Muslims..." Thus European countries were not alone in the belief of their divine right, as members of God's community, over non-believers and their lands.

The historian Nicholas Canny[8] noted that during the Elizabethan conquest of Ireland, circa 1560-1570, the English had little hesitation in declaring the Gaelic Irish

> ...to be pagan...the English were decreeing that they were culpable since their heathenism was owing not to a lack of opportunity but rather to the fact that their system of government was antithetical to Christianity. Once it was established that the Irish were pagans, the first logical step had been taken toward declaring them barbarians. The English were able to pursue their argument further when they witnessed the appearance of the native Irish, their habits, customs and agricultural methods.

Christianity and its Judaic roots provided the legitimizing foundation for this process. Mosaic canon provided the body of law that encompassed these new lands and its inhabitants. The colonies of Massachusetts Bay and later Connecticut[9] cited a single scriptural foundation for the laws issued by these respective governments which addressed not only land issues, but also their entire body of law. The Book of Romans in the New Testament (Chapter 13, verses 1, 2) provided this body of law with a divine sanction:

> Let every Soul be subject to the Higher Powers; for there is no Power but of God, the Powers that be are Ordained of God.
>
> Whosoever therefore resisteth the Power resisteth the Ordinance of God: and they that resist, shall receive to themselves Damnation.

Thus John Winthrop, the first governor of Massachusetts Bay Colony, was able to declare that the region's non-Christian, non-sedentary Indian inhabitants were not among the "sonnes of men" to whom the Lord had given dominion over the Earth,

> And for the natives of New England they enclose noe Land neither have noe settled habitation nor any tame Cattel to improve the land by & soe have noe other but a naturall right to those countries Soe as if we leave them suffficent fore theire use wee may lawfully take the rest theire being more than enough for them & us.[10]

Winthrop's sentiments were echoed in the writings of the Reverend John Cotton (1636),[11]

> ...it was neither the Kings intendment, nor the English Planters to take possession of the Countrey by murther of the Natives, or by robbery: but either to take possession of the voyd places of the Countrey by the Law of Nature, (for *Vacuum Domicilium credit occupanti*) or if we tooke any Lands from the Natives, it was by way of purchase, and free consent.

In his 1823 Supreme Court opinion (*Johnson and Graham's Lessee v William M'Intosh*),[12] Chief Justice John Marshall concurred with the concept of *Title by Discovery*,

> In this first effort made by the English government to acquire territory on this continent, we perceive a complete recognition of the principle which has been mentioned [*title by discovery*]. The right of discovery given by this commission, is to countries "then unknown to Christian

people"; and of these countries Cabot was empowered to take possession in the name of the king of England. Thus asserting the right to take possession notwithstanding the occupancy of the natives, who were heathens...

The distinction between the *Naturall right* (at times referred to as *aboriginal right* or *Indian title*) of the Indians to the land they occupied at the time of discovery, and the legal title of the English crown to sovereignty was clearly defined. The sovereign held the legal title to the lands, while the Indians retained only usufructuary rights or rights of occupancy.

The Jesuit Scholar Francis Prucha summed up the European rationale underlying this process when, in his exhaustive study of Anglo-Indian relations,[13] he stated:

> ...the English colonies did not simply dispossess the Indians as though they had no right of any kind to the land. The vast claims in the New World made by European monarchs on the slightest pretense of "discovery" were claims against other European monarchs, not against the aboriginal inhabitants of those lands, and the handsome grants made to trading companies or individual proprietors in the form of colonial charters were of the same nature...absolute dominion or sovereignty over the land rested in the European nations or their successors, leaving to the aborigines the possessory and usufructuary rights to the land they occupied and used.

As a result of this distinction between fee title and rights of occupancy we find a continual motif present in documents pertaining to the establishment of Indian reserves: that lands were being "set aside for their use," "sufficient for their needs," or "planting," thereby fulfilling the requirements of "Natural right."

The discovery of the lands, including those bounding on Long Island Sound, by Cabot while sailing under his 1496 patent, which later became the Connecticut colony, laid the legal foundation upon which the colonies of both Plymouth and Massachusetts Bay, and later Connecticut, were to lay claim to fee title, in the King's name, to all the lands encompassed by their own respective charters. This discovery left the native inhabitants of the lands within these colonies with only, as Prucha termed: "possessory and usufructuary" privileges. In English law, the term *tenants at will* was used. This classification continued during both the American colonial and federalist historical periods for lands encompassed originally by colonial grants and which later became states. The United States Congress explicitly maintained this position as noted in the following 1796 (April) debate on the Federal Indian Trade and Non-Intercourse Act[14] in the U.S. House of Representatives,

> By the theory of the British law all titles to the soil were originally in the King; he was lord paramount and all lands not immediately disposed of by the Crown, within his extensive dominions were vested in him. The savages of these Provinces' when under the British Government were considered a conquered people, and tenants at will. And hence they were unable to convey, unless previously admitted by the Crown, and then their title was their right of occupancy, and not the dignity of a fee simple, the King's grant being necessary to vest the fee...
> ...At the Treaty of Peace in 1783, it was acknowledged that the representative States were the fee sovereigns of all the lands contained within their Provincial charters, which placed them in the precise situation with respect to the fee His Majesty had previously done in fee simple...
> ...the Indians therefore, were tenants at will, and not tenants in possession of a fee simple estate. To prove this, also, they have ever been incapable of conveying their estate, not even for life, without leave of Government. Inheritance and alienation were incident to a fee...

These principles of law were advanced by King James in his 1612 grant known as the "Great Patent of New England" to the "said council called the council established at Plimouth." The King granted these individual investors "all that part of North America, called New England, from the 40 to the 48gr.of North Latitude...Pemmaquid" (Maine south to Delaware Bay), "the aforesayd part of America, lyeing & being in breath from 40 degrees of northerly latitude from the equinoctial line to forty-eight degrees of sayd northerly latitude...throughout the maine land from sea to sea" not to include any lands "actually possessed or inhabited bye any Christian Prince or state" (*Terra nullus*). This grant was foundational to the legitimacy of eastern Long Island towns, including Southampton.

In 1628, King Charles I assumed the throne of England, adjourned or suspended Parliament, and set in motion the Calvinist exodus to the New World. It was during 1628 that John Endicott and several other investors purchased a portion of the 1612 'Great Patent' from the Council of Plymouth, had it reconfirmed by King Charles I, and by 1630 had established the Massachusetts Bay Colony. On March 3, 1636 the General Court of Massachusetts granted a commission to Thomas Hooker, John Winthrop Jr., Roger Ludlow and other "...ffreemen & members of Newe Towne, Dorchestr, Waterton, & other places, whoe are resolved to transplant themselues & their estates unto the Ryver Conecticott, there to reside & inhabite."[15] This commission in turn gave the incipient Connecticut colony its pre-1662 legal basis to exercise judicial authority to issue not only land grants but also to obtain land from the region's Indians independent of the Massachusetts Bay General Court,

> ...under the greater part of their hands, at a day or dayes by them appointed, upon convenient notice, to convene the said

inhabitants of the towns to any convenient place they shall think meete, in a legal and open manner, by way of court, to procede in executing the power and authority aforesaid.[16]

As Andrews further noted,[17]

> The Supreme authority in the Commonwealth was the General Court. It was given power "to make lawes or reapeale them, to grant levies, to admit of Freeman, dispose of Lands undisposed of to Several towns or Persons, to call either Court or Magistrate or any other Person whatsoever into question for any misdemeanor....

By way of summary, England was able to claim title to the lands of New England by *Right of Discovery*. Discovery to be interpreted as lands occupied under a certain set of conditions that were present (the occupants were not Christian, they did not practice animal husbandry, they did not reside in settled locations) at the time of their first discovery by an agent commissioned by a Christian king. At this point in time and under those conditions, a Christian king could legally claim full title to the lands, leaving the land's occupants (the Indians) with only occupancy or aboriginal rights to the lands.

The Earl's Domain

The Council of New England was the successor name for the Council of Plymouth, the patentee of the 1612 "Great Patent of New England." It was noted earlier that the Massachusetts Bay Company purchased a portion of that grant from the Council of Plymouth, essentially all of present day Maine, New Hampshire, Massachusetts, Rhode Island, and Connecticut.[18] In 1635, "by and with ye consent, direction, appointment, and command of his most Sacred majesty the King,"[19] the Council of New England granted to Lord William Alexander, the Earl of Stirling a portion of the remaining grant lands including all of Long Island,[20]

Patent given by the Plymouth Company to William Alexander, the Earl of Sterling. April 20, 1635.

To all xpian people unto whome this pnts shall come The COUNCELL for the affaires of Newe England send Greetings in our Lord God everlasting Whereas our late Sovraigne Lord King James of blessed memory by his highness Letters Patents under the Great Seale of England bearinge Date att Westmonister the Third daye of November in the Eighteenth yeare of his Maties Raigne over his higness Realme of England for the considerations in the said Letters Patent expressed and declared hath absolutely givn graunted and confirmed unto the said Counsell and theire Successors for ever, all that land of Newe England in America lyinge and beinge in breath from fortie degrees of Northerly latitude from the Equinoctiall Lyne to fortie eight degrees of the said Northerly latitude inclusivelie and in length of and within all the breadth aforesaid throughout the maine Land from Sea to Sea...the Islands and Seas adjoyninge...NOWE KNOWE all men by these pnts that the said Councell of Newe England in America beinge assembled in publique Courte accordinge to an Acte made and agreed uppon the third day of February last past before the date of theis pnts for divers good causes and consideracons them hereunto especially movinge HAVE given graunted alienated bargained and sold And in and by theis pnts doe for them and theire Successors give graunt alien bargaine sell and confirme unto the Right Honorable William Lord Alexander his heirs and assignes All that part of the maine Land of Newe England aforesaid ...*alsoe all that Island or Islands heretofore commonly called by severall name or names of Matowa or Longe Island and hereafter to be called be the name of the Isle of Starlinge lyinge and being to the Westward of Cape Codd or the Narohigansets*... (emphasis added).[21]

Having obtained a portion as stated above of the 1612 grant made by James I to the Plymouth Company, Lord William Alexander, Earl of Stirling, gained undisputed title in the King's name to the lands of Long Island.

The "inhabitants of Linne" and the Earl's Patent

Other than supplying colonists, the Massachusetts Bay Colony had little to do with obtaining lands or the establishment of a settlement at what was to become known as Southampton. From the beginning, the Bay Colony had no legal jurisdiction on Long Island. Secondary sources do agree however that the bulk of Southampton's original colonists came from the Lynn, Massachusetts and Boston areas.[22] Primary sources (Essex Quarter Court records, Lynn Quarter Court records, Massachusetts Bay General Court records) support these claims. As Governor John Winthrop noted in 1640: "divers of the inhabitants of Linne, finding themselves straitened looked out for a new plantation; and so going to Long Island, they agreed with Lord Starling's agent there, one Mr Forrett..."[23] "Forret" was James Farrett, Lord Alexander's New England agent. Alexander, the Earl of Stirling possessing the King's patent for Long Island, was the person these "inhabitants of Linne" had to deal with in order to establish a legal plantation there. Farrett in consultation with Alexander, Earl of Stirling, obtained the Earl's approval in August of 1639 for a conveyance of a portion of his Long Island holdings to these future proprietors,

> Lord Stirling's Confirmation to Convey the Lands of His Royal Patent at Southampton. August 20, 1639.

> I William Earle of Sterling doe make knowne to all men to whom it doth or may concerne, that whereas James Farret Gent, my lawful Agent upon Long Island &c in America hath disposed by sale of divers lands in my name and for my use upon the said Island and Islands adjacent within my pattent according to the power given him by myselfe, April 1637, unto Edward Howell Daniel Howe, and their heirs and successours for ever as from Peaconnet to ye easternmost poynte of ye said Long Island: and unto John Thomas, and Edward Farington and successively to the longest liver of

them and to his heirs and assignes for ever: I say whatsoever bargaine of Paumanucke, with his son Weeayacombon and their associates; that is Sassgotacon, Checanoe and Mauneehen on the other side Lion Gardener for himselfe his contract and conclusion the above named parties (for themselves heirs and assignes for ever) have made with Mr. Faret, according to the custom of New England, I the said Wm Earle of Sterline ratifie and hold of value in law: and doe upon the request of my said Agent James Faret by these presents bind my selfe heirs assignes to doe any further act or thing whereby or wherewith ye titles of ye above named parties (vizt) Howell, How, Farringtones, Sunderland, and their heirs and successors for ever, may be strengthened, wch they have under the hand and seale of my aforesaid Agent James Faret, of wch I am by him fully satisfied: and that he hath in full satisfaction for the said lands for my use received a competent sum of money, in consideration of wch money, I doe acquit all right title interest and demand of and to ye sd lands and patent right for ever.

Witness my hand and seale this twentieth day of August one thousand six hundred thirty-nine

signed Stirline[24]

Farrett, as the Earl's agent, having received the above confirmation, issued a conditional deed of conveyance in his own name for "eight miles square of land or soe..." to the named proprietors (the original investors). Conferred within this document was the right to purchase Indian occupancy rights in their own names,

Deed of James Farrett. April 17, 1640.

Know all men whom this present writing may concerne that I James ffaret of Long Island Gent Deputy to the right honrbl the Earl of Starling Secretary for the kingdom of Scotland doe by these prsents in the name and behalf of the said Earle and in mine own name allsoe as his Deputy as it doth or may any way concerne myself, Give and grant free leave and liberty to Daniell How, Job Sayre, George Wilby and William Harker together with their associates to sitt downe upon Long Island aforesaide, there to possess improve and enjoy eight miles square of land or soe much as shall containe the said quantity not only upland but alsoe whatsoever meadow marish ground, harbors, Rivrs and creeks lye within the bounds or limits of the said eight miles, The same and every part thereof quietly and peaceably to enjoy to them and their heyres forever without any disturbance, lett or molestation from the said earle or any by his appoyntment or prcurement for him or any of his. And that they are to take their choise to sit down upon the best lyketh them and alsoe that they and their associates shall enjoy as full and free liberty in all matters that doe or may concerne them or theirs or that may conduce to ye good and comfort of them and theirs both in church order and civill Government together with all other Easmts conveniences and accommodations whatsoever which the said place doth or may afford, answerable to what other plantations enjoy in Massachusetts Bay. But in as much as it hath pleased our Royall King to Give and grant the patent of long Island to the aforesaid Earle: In consideration thereof it is agreed upon that the trade with ye Indians shall remaine to ye said Earle of Starling to Dispose of from time to time and at all times as best liketh him. ...ffurther it is agreed up on that noe man shall by vertue of any gift or purchase lay any claime to any land lying within the compass of the eight miles before mentioned but onely the afforesaid Inhabitants shall make purchase (in theire owne names at theire owne leisure from any Indians that Inhabit or have lawful right to any of the aforesaid land) all or any pt thereof, and thereby assure it to themselves and their heyres as theire inheritance for ever. In witness whereof wee hereunto set our hands and seales the 17th day of Aprill, 1640.[25]

The following August, Farrett provided yet another document for the Southampton proprietors. It was a confirmation of the conveyance in which the actual land boundaries of the plantation were clearly defined,

Confirmation by James Farrett. July 7, 1640.[26]

Memorandum: It is agreed upon between James Ffaret agent, and Edward Howell, John Gosmer, Edmund Ffarington, Daniel Howe, Thomas Halsey, Edward Needham, Allen Breed, Thomas Sayre, Henry Walton, George Welby, William Harker, and Job Sayre: that whereupon it is agreed upon a covenant passed between us touching the extent of a planacon in Long Island, that the aforesaid Mr. Edward Howell and his copartners shall enjoy eight miles square of land or so much as the said eight miles shall containe, and that now lie in said bounds being laid out and agreed upon: It is to begin at a place westward from Shinecock entitled the name of the place where the Indians drawe over their cannoes out of the north bay over to the south side of the island, and from there to run along that neck of land eastward the whole breadth between the bays aforesaid to the easterly end of an Island or neck of land lying over against the Island commonly known by the name of Mr. Ffarret's Islad [present-day Shelter Island], To enjoy all and every parte there of according as yt is expressed in our agreement elsewhere, with that Island or neck lying over against Mr Ffarret's Island formerly expressed.

James Farret

Thomas Dexter
Richard Walker
Witnesses

The plantation at Southampton now found itself with a chain of legal title from the King of England through the Council of New England to the Earl of Stirling to the proprietors of Southampton.

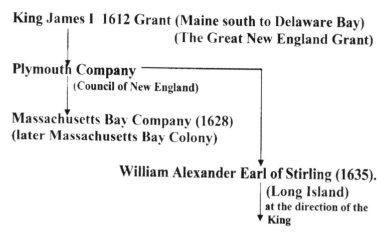

Southampton Proprietors
(1640)

    The lands constituting the plantation of Southampton were initially to the east of "the place where the Indians drawe over their canoes out of the north bay over to the south side of the Island," the present-day Canoe Place Canal.
    Southampton not only became a town, but also a "mini-colony" in its own right with its own General Court. Yet Southampton represented an anomaly, a threatened anomaly. Southampton was a town, but not part of a royal colony or province. The lands upon which it was settled were still claimed by the Dutch authorities at New Amsterdam.[27] It thus lacked the protection and recognition of other neighboring colonies. As a first step in their effort to remedy this, the Southampton proprietors sought the recognition of their legal status from the neighboring colony of Massachusetts. On the same day that James Farrett presented the Town Proprietors with his confirmation of his deed of conveyance, the Town also obtained the endorsement and recognition by Governor

Beginnings

John Winthrop of the conveyance from Lord Stirling to the Proprietors of Southampton,

> Governor John Winthrop's Endorsement of Lord Stirling's Patent Conveyance by James Farrett. August 20, 1640.[28]
>
> I John Winthrop within named having seriously considered of that within this writing is refered to my determination althought I am unwilling to take it upon mee and as unfit alsoe the rather being to seeke of any rule or approved president to guide me herein yet being called hereunto: I shall express what Ai conceive to be Equall upon the considerations here ensueing, viz. The land within granted being a mere wilderness and the natives of the place pretending some interest which ye planters must purchase, And they might have land enough gratis (and as convenient) in ye Massachusetts or other of the Collines with liberte to trade with the Indians (which they are debarred from) And for that they had possessed and improved this place before any actual claime made thereto by the rt honrble the Earle of Starling or had any notice of his Lopps pattent, And whereas his Lopp (for consideration I suppose of the prmises) requires nothing of them but in a way of acknowledgement of his Interest, I doe here upon conceive and doe accordingly (so farre as power is given mee) order and set down that the Inhabitants of the tract of land within mentioned or the plantation now called Southampton upon Long Island, and their successors for ever shall pay yearly to the said Earle of Starling his heyres or assignes upon the last day of September at Southampton aforesaid four bushels of the best Indian corne there growing or the value soe much in full satisfaction of all rents and services (the 5th pt of gold and silver ore to the King's maties reserved always excepted) In testimony whereof I have hereunto set my hand. Dated 20th (8) 1640.

Yet this document did not provide sufficient protection for the town. Other decisions had to be made and other actions taken.

"as may be most sutable to theire own comforts"

At a Proprietor's meeting held at Southampton on March 7, 1644, the Town was notified that the Connecticut General Court had voted and accepted Southampton into its jurisdiction.[29] Both the Colony and the Town entered (1643) into an agreement to effectuate this union,

> ...Ye Combynation of Southampton wth Harford[30]
>
> Whereas formerly sume Oureters have by letters paste betwixt sum deputed by the Jurissdiction of Conectecote and other of ye plantation of Southampton upon Long Iland concerning union into one body and gouernment, whereby ye said Towne might be interested in ye general combination of ye united Collonies, for prosecution and issuing wherof, Edward Hopkins & John Haines being authorized wth said powers from ye Generall Corte for ye jurisdiction of Conecticute, & Edward Howell, John Gosmore and John More deputed by ye Towne of Soutampton, It was by the said parties concluded & agreed, And ye said Towne of Southampton doe by theire said deputies, for themselves and theire successors, assotiate and joyne themselves to ye jurisdiction of Conecticote, to be subject to al lawes there established, and accoding to ye word of God and right reson, wth such exceptions & limitations as are hereafter expressed...

Due to Southampton's isolated location, this agreement of union contained an unusual, but important provision, which granted the Town the ability to govern itself, subject to certain conditions:

> ...It [is] agreed and concluded, yt if upon vewe of such orders as are alreddy established by ye General Court for ye jurisdiction of Connectecoate, there be found any difference therein from such as are also for ye present settled in ye Towne of Southampton, the said Towne shal have liberite to regulate themselues according as may be most sutable to theire own comforts and conueniences in theire own

judgment, provided those orders made by them concerne themselues only and intrence not upon ye interests of others of ye Generall Combination of ye united Collonies, and not cross to ye rule of riteousness. The like power is also reserved unto themselves for the future, for making of such orders as may concerne theire Town ocations...."[31]

In their September 1644 meeting held at Hartford, the Commissioners for the United Colonies in New England sanctioned the conditions and act of union.[32]

Therefore, of all the towns and plantations under Connecticut's jurisdiction, Southampton had the most liberal association with the Colony. As long as the Town did not enact laws in violation of Holy Scripture or infringe upon the interests of any neighboring towns, and as long as the Town paid taxes due to the Colony, the Proprietors and Freemen of Southampton were essentially free to govern themselves. In 1649, the Proprietors of the Town of East Hampton followed suit and also united themselves with the Colony.[33]

Thus by 1650, Southampton had only one established town on her boundaries, East Hampton to her east.

King Charles II, in his 1662 Charter to Connecticut included all "the Islands thereunto adioyneinge."[34] The Connecticut General Court of Elections declared "that they claim Long Island as one of those adjoining Islands expressed in the Charter, except a precedent right doth appear, approved by his Majesty."[35]

No royally sanctioned precedent ever emerged nor was one claimed by any other political entity save the Dutch at New Amsterdam. The Town's title to all lands within its boundaries was thus perfected, that is, declared in complete compliance with English law, by Charles II's Patent.

In summary, Southampton's proprietors' rights to their lands were initially derived from Lord Stirling's Patent. Soon after acquiring this right they sought and acquired the legal protection afforded by becoming subject to the jurisdiction of Connecticut Colony. As indicated above, the terms under which they joined the Colony were exceedingly liberal for the times: "said Towne shal have liberite to regulate themselues according as may be most sutable to theire own comforts and conueniences in theire own judgment…"

II. The "Seponark Indians" and their Lands

To call the Shinnecock a tribe at the time of first sustained contact with Europeans would be a misnomer. As with other Indian groups, both in central and eastern Long Island, the Indians that became known to the Europeans as the Shinnecock consisted of several quasi-independent kinship related bands that were initially referred to by the Town as the "Seponark Indians."[1] These Indians occupied a generalized land base that stretched from present day Appacock Creek on the west, eastward to Wainscott, the present-day boundary between the towns of Southampton and East Hampton. East of them were the Montauk Indians.

In time, as a result of continual interactions with the local colonial and provincial authorities, these quasi-independent groups coalesced into a single political entity unified under its own leadership. The term "Shinnecock," an Algonquian dialectical term meaning "at the level land or country,"[2] was a geographical reference to the lands that these various bands occupied. In time this geographical appellation became associated with its native occupants. In the present, the term has also been applied to the neck of land within Southampton that has become the home to the Shinnecock.

In turn, these proto-Shinnecock bands were, at the time of European contact, closely related; both culturally, linguistically, and politically with other similar Indian groups on the eastern end of Long Island. There were groups collectively known as the "Yeanacocks" that occupied an area where the present day Peconic River empties into Peconic Bay in the Town of Riverhead.

A second group, known as the "Curchaug" occupied a land area from present-day Wading River to Orient Point encompassing the present-day towns of Riverhead (excepting that area occupied by the Yeanacocks) and Southold, that is, the North Fork of Long Island.

On the South Fork of the Island resided the "Montauk" who occupied the lands east of those associated with the Shinnecock to present-day Montauk Point.

Lastly, there were the "Manhassets" who occupied Shelter Island which lay upon Peconic Bay between the North and South Forks of eastern Long Island. At the time of early contact, the Manhassets were at the center of political control over the Indian groups occupying eastern Long Island.

Culturally, all of these Indian groups were very similar. All four exploited their environment in the same manner, with scattered kin-based villages, seasonally-based subsistence activities based upon hunting and gathering, maritime resources, and agriculture. The linguistic dialect of the Algonquian language spoken amongst these peoples was the same. This particular dialect was closely related to those Indian groups that occupied southeastern Connecticut and southwestern Rhode Island (the Niantic and Narragansett). It is suggestive of the pre-contact origin of these Indian groups now residing on eastern Long Island.[3]

What is especially noteworthy was the political relationship present between all of these groups including the Shinnecock. As early as 1636, there was evidence that the Indian groups on eastern Long Island were under the political domination of one particular kin group. Lion Gardner, in his 1636 narrative of the Pequot War[4] noted that three days after the battle with the Pequots at Mystic Fort in Connecticut, Gardner was approached by Wiandance, the sachem or chief of the Montauk whom he described as "Wiandance, next brother to the old Sachem of Long Island." Wiandance then stated to Gardner, "I will go to my brother, for he is the great Sachem of all Long Island...." When Gardner later visited Wiandance on Long Island, he noted that "then they went to Shelter Island, where the old Sachem dwelt—Wiandance's older brother..." Gardner later noted regarding Wiandance, that, "the brother of this Sachem was Shinacock Sachem...." Three of the four identifiable Indian groups are here identified as being led by members of one kinship group, that is, three brothers, the oldest of whom ascribed to the status of "sachem of Paumonoc."[5] His name is given as "Yovawan" (c.1639) (aka "Youghcoe," "Poggatacut," "Pomotuck"). All four brothers are named in the Plymouth Colony Records,[6] "Youghco, Wiantance, Moughmaitow, Weenakamin [the sachem over the Shinnecock]."

At the time of Wiandance's 1636 visit to Gardner at Old Saybrook, he and the Montauk also became deeply involved in the colonists' conflict with the Pequot, a tribe that had caused problems for the Montauk for many years. Wiandance, along with a group of Montauk warriors, assisted the colonial forces in hunting down remnants of the Pequot who fled westward, along the Connecticut coastline towards New Amsterdam. This pursuit culminated in the "Great Swamp Fight" in present-day Southport, Connecticut. Wiandance fought alongside Gardner in this conflict. Wiandance has been credited with saving Gardnier's life in this battle. The two remained close friends for the rest of their lives. Wiandance later spent a significant amount of time at the plantation at Old Saybrook, becoming well acquainted with the English there and their culture. It was this basis of knowledge and experience among the colonists that Wiandance later shared as the Long Island chief sachem with the Shinnecock and other Indian groups on eastern Long Island. He and the Montauk warriors with him became agents of acculturation and change amongst the Indians of eastern Long Island.

The assumption of this role as the leading kin group over the Indians of eastern Long Island may have been linked to the conquest by the Montauk of the three other Indian groups. A story was recounted circa 1670 to Daniel Denton[7] which mentioned the Montauk conquest of the Shinnecock Indians. In the aftermath, the Montauk sachem, "Mongotucksee" had his son take a Shinnecock woman, the daughter of the Shinnecock sachem, to wife, thus establishing both a kinship bond and political relationship between the two peoples.

Although Yovawan and his successor Wiandance, who assumed this role after Yovawam's death in 1641, asserted political dominance over the Shinnecock, day to day affairs were left to a leading band sub-sachem who was answerable to Wiandance and his successor, his son "Wiacombie" ("Wyacombone").[8] His son died prematurely and was succeeded by "Weany Sunk" (Sunk Squaw) (1662), variously described in documents as Wiandance's widow, sister, or daughter. The preponderance of primary source records described her as his spouse.[9]

The early Southampton records mention "Mandush" (aka "Nowedanoh")[10] acting in that sub-sachem leadership capacity for the Shinnecock. In 1674 he was succeeded by his son "Pungamo."[11] By 1703 the Shinnecock leadership had politically evolved into a tripartite form with three band sachems: "Pungamo, Gice, Mamanamon."[12]

Indian Land Conveyances and Connecticut Laws: 1639–1668

At the heart of the relationship between the Town of Southampton and the Shinnecock Indians were the lands. As was noted earlier, within three days of their arrival from Massachusetts, the new colonists had reached an agreement with the Shinnecock over particular lands upon which they could establish their plantation. They formally acquired the

The "Seponark Indians" and their Lands

Indian title to these lands in 1640. They did so under right of their acquisition of title right from Lord Stirling,

> This indenture, made the 13th day of Decembe, Anno Dom. 1640, between Pomatuck, Mandush, Mocomanto, Pathemanto, Wybbennett, Wainmenowog, Heden, Watemexoted, Checkepuchat, the native inhabitants & true owners of the eastern pt. of Long Island on the one part, and Mr. John Gosmer, Edward Howell, Daniell How, Edward Needham, Thomas Halsey, John Cooper, Thomas Sayre, Edward Ffarington, Job Sayre, George Welbee, Allen Breade, Will'm Harker, Henry Walton, on the other part, witnesseth that the sayd Indians for due consideration of sixteene coats already received, and alsoe three score bushels of Indian corne to bee payed upon lawful demand the last of September, which shall be in the yeare 1641, & further in consideration that the above named English shall defend vs the sayd Indians from the unjust violence of whatever Indians shall illegally assail vs. doe absolutely & for ever give & grant & by these presents doe acknowledge ourselves, to have given & granted to the parties above mentioned, without any fraud, guile, mentall reservation or equivocation to them &theire heirs & successors for ever, all the lands, woods, waters, water courses, easements, profits, & emoluments thence arisinge what soever from the place commonly knowne by the place where the Indians hayle over their canoes out of the north bay to the South side of the Island, from thence to pocess all the lands lying eastward between the aforesaid bounds by water, to wit, all the lands pertaining to the parteyes aforesaid, as alsoe all the old ground formerly planted lying eastward from the first creek at the west-more end of Shinecock plaine, to have and to hold forever without any claime or challenge of the least title, interest or propriety whatsoever of vs the sayd Indianbs or our heyres or sucessors or by any others by our leave, appointment liencse counsel or authority whatsoever, all the land bounded as is above said. In full testimonie of this our absolute bargaine, contract,& grant indented & in full& complete satisfaction & establishment of this our act & deed of passing over all our

title and interest in the premises, with all emoluments & profits thereto appertaining or any wise belonging from sea or land within our limits above specified without all guile wee have set to our hands the day and yeare above sayd.

Memorand. Before the subscribing of this present writing it is agreed that the Indians above named have libertie to break up ground for theire use to the westward of the creek aforementioned on the west side of Shinecock plaine.

Manatact, Mandush, Wybenet, Howes, Secommecock, Mocomanto, these in the name of the rest.

By this deed instrument the plantation's proprietors acquired the Shinnecock's aboriginal or Indian title to the lands lying between Canoe Place ("the place where the Indians hayle their canoes") on the west to Shinnecock Plains (Wainscott, "Old Ground") on the east from Long Island Sound south to the Atlantic Ocean. It is also noted that the first Indian signatory subscribing to the act was "Pomatuck" (Yovawan) the sachem over eastern Long Island. The second subscribing signatory was "Mandush," the sub-sachem of the Shinnecock. This tells us that Mandush did not have the authority to convey any land rights on his own volition. It required Yovawam's approval and approbation. That this was clearly the situation was confirmed in the 1666 affidavit of Thomas Halsey, a Southampton proprietor, wherein Wiandance, now the superior sachem (sagamore) of eastern Long Island participated in a ritual signifying such a status.[13]

> I the subscribed namely Thomas Halsey doe witness, that at the time of trouble in this towne of Southampton by reason of murder committed by the Indians, At a great assembly of the Indians for the settling of matters, in fine I saw Mandush (whoe was a man repnted & acknowledged generally by all Indians in those parts to bee the great sachems sonne of Shinecock) cutt up a turf of ground in Southampton, and delivering it to Wyandanch gave up all his right and interest unto him, And hee the said Mandush with many other of the

chiefee of Shinecock Indians as ancient men, did manifest their consent and that they contented, by their ordinary signe of stroaking Wyandanch on the back, And since that time the said Wyandancd (who was sachem of Meantauk) hath acted upon ye aforesaid Interest given to him as by letting and disposing of land at Quaquanantuck and else where And I never heard of any deny Wyandanch his right and propriety in the premies until of late, And this I am ready to depose when there unto called, Witness my hand and this 19 of Sept. 1666,

This ritual, the stroking of Wiandance's back by the Shinnecock elders, was common both on Long Island and the mainland. It was known as *Cowaunckamish*, "my service to you" as signified by the stroking of the sachems shoulders.[14] This stroking ritual signified subservience to the one being stroked.

With this 1641 cession, in conformity with contemporary English law, and with the approbation of the pertinent Indian authorities (Pomatuck's), Southampton, as an independent plantation, acquired a perfected land title to the land area described in the deed. What is also of importance was the fact that the English proprietors and Pomatuck worked to ensure that the Indians themselves were not to be deprived lands upon which to produce foodstuffs, "…agreed that the Indians above named have libertie to break up ground for theire use to the westward of the creek aforementioned on the west side of Shinecock plaine." It is clear that the Town did not intend to expel the Indians residing within Southampton's bounds.

In 1643 Southampton came under the jurisdiction of the Colony of Connecticut. At this point the Town became subject to that colony's laws, including those laws concerning land title acquisition, subject to the special stipulations granted to the Town by the Connecticut General Court of Elections.

Under Connecticut's laws, Indians living in tribal relations within Connecticut Colony retained only *occupancy or aboriginal rights* that could be extinguished either by purchase (conveyance of right) or by right of conquest resulting from justifiable hostilities (as in the case of the Pequot War which affected the lands of the Pequot and Pequannock tribes).[15]

Indians residing within the colony were also given equal protection under the law. As early as 1639, the Connecticut General Court declared: "all persons in this colony, whether inhabitants or not, should enjoy the same law and justice without partiality or delay."[16] Thus Indians holding tenancy rights could not be summarily removed from lands that they had no desire to convey and, in essence, reserved to themselves.

The Indian occupants could, and did, convey such parcels, exchange them for other parcels, or simply abandon them and move out of the area. In this latter case, plantation lands previously occupied by Indians would be considered vacant (vacuum domicilium) and relegated to the status of undivided proprietary common land available for future division.

Connecticut, from the begining prohibited the acquisition by individuals of Indian occupancy rights.[17]

> Whereas there is an order of Courte amoungst us wch prohibititts all perticular persons within this Jurisdiction rom buying any lands of the Indians, either directly or ndirectly, under any pretense whatsoever.

In Connecticut the extinguishment of Indian occupancy rights was commonly accomplished by use of a committee representing a town's proprietors. These committees had to negotiate with the Indians for particular tracts of land. The parties had to arrive at a mutually agreeable settlement and each had to appear before a town magistrate, later known as a Justice of the Peace, to attest to the conveyance and to confirm that they were entering into the transaction of "theire own free act and deed." The magistrate, as an officer of the General Court would, as required by law, affix his approbating signature to the document signifying the Court's conditional approbation to the conveyance.[18]

The local magistrate representing the General Court was charged with ensuring compliance with all Colonial laws applicable to the parties involved. This explains the necessity for his signature upon deeds of conveyance certifying, as the *juristic persona* of the General Court, that the conveyance was in compliance with all applicable laws.

A copy of the conveyance would be transcribed by the town Recorder or Clerk into the town records as required by law. The original document containing the Colony's approbation remained in the custody of the Colony.[19]

By issuing a proprietary grant, the Colony usually conferred upon the grantees the authority to obtain from the Indians (i.e., to extinguish) their usufructuary or aboriginal rights to all the lands encompassed by the grant. As the General Court noted:[20]

> that every Townships Grants of Lands, as they have been obtained by gift, purchase or otherwise of the Natives and grant this Court may be settled upon them, their Heirs, Successors and Assigns for ever, according to our Charter granted by His Late Majesty of happy memory.

That is, once a town, made a legal acquisition of *Indian title* (aboriginal right) to any lands within a town, that land according to the Colony's Charter could not be taken or alienated from that town.

Yet, as we have seen, Southampton's situation was unique. Obtaining a portion of the Stirling Patent lands in actuality created an independent "mini" colony. Southampton, prior to its union with Connecticut, had its own General Court and enacted its own laws. It obtained the lands within its original granted area via deeds approbated by its own proprietary government. Farrett's, deed of April 17, 1640, given in the name of Lord Stirling, clearly conveyed the right of the Town's "undertakers" or proprietary investors to obtain the aboriginal or native right to lands within the purchase bounds. The conveyance of such aboriginal right was made by the Shinnecock in the December 13, 1640 deed to the Town proprietors. The instrument itself was typical, with the Shinnecock tribal leadership as grantors, the proprietors as grantees and the act itself being subscribed to and witnessed by members of both parties.

As we have also seen, elements of Southampton's original independence remained, and were part of, the 1643 agreement of union with Connecticut:

> the said Towne shal have liberite to regulate themselues according as may be most sutable to theire own comforts and conueniences in theire own judgment, provided those orders made by them concerne themselues only and intrence not upon ye interests of others of ye Generall Combination of ye united Collonies, and not cross to ye rule of riteousness. The like power is also reserved unto themselves for the future, for making of such orders as may concerne theire Town ocations....

Thus, on the basis of the terms of agreement, Southampton could expand her original boundaries if she felt the need, provided the action did not infringe upon the rights of any established town or English colony. At the same time Southampton, like any other Connecticut town, was bound by Colony law to acquire such lands in a legally sanctioned manner as described below:[21]

> This Court orders, that no person in this Colony shall buy, hire, or receive as a gift or mortgage, any parcel of land or lands of any Indian or Indians, for the future, except he doe

buy or receive the same for the use of the Colony or the benefitt of some Towne with the allowance of the Court.

From this point forward until 1662, when the Town was forced to become part of the Province of New York, all land acquisitions between the Town of Southampton and the Shinnecock had to be in conformity with Connecticut law. The salient point here was that individuals residing in the colony were strictly prohibited from directly purchasing Indian lands unless authorized to do so by either the Town or the General Court.

While the manner of purchase of Indian title was clearly proscribed by the Colony, an ambiguous situation did exist. Only two Long Island towns were then under Connecticut's jurisdiction, Southampton and East Hampton. The lands on the western boundary of Southampton were claimed by both England and the Dutch.[22] They were in essence, from a legal standpoint, a no-man's land. An example of this situation and the ambiguity of the situation was the nature of the land acquisition that is, a conditional rental/conveyance by Wiandance to his friend Lion Gardner of beach land and meadows in the lands to the west of Southampton on June 10, 1658,[23]

> Be it knowne to all men by this present writing, that this indenture covenant or agreemenr was made this tenth day of June in theyeare of our Lord one thousand six hundred fifty and eight betweene Wiandance, Sachem heirs, executors, and assignes, that is to say that the aforesaid Sachem Wiadance; hath sold for a considerable summe of money and goods a certaine tract of beach land with all the rest of the grasse that joins to it and not separated from it by the water, which beach begins eastwards at the west end of Southampton bounds and westwards were it is separated by the water; the sea coming out of the ocean sea; being bounded south-wards by the great sea; north-wards by the inland water; this land and the grasse thereof for a range or run for to feed horses or cattell on; I say

I have sold to the aforesaid Lion Gardener his heirs executors or assigns forever for the sum aforesayd and a yearly rent of twenty-five shillings a yeare; which yearly rent is to be paid to the aforesaid Sachem his heirs, executors and assigns for ever in the eight month called October then to be demanded, but the whales that shall be casted upon this beach shall belong to me and the rest of my Indians in theire bounds as they have been anciently granted to them formerly by my forefathers, and alsoe liberty to cut in the summertime bullrushes and such things as they make theire matts of, provided they do no hurt to the horses that is thereon and that this writing is to be understood according to the letter with out any reservation or further interpretation on it we have both of us interchangeably set to our hands and seals

Lion Gardener

Signed sealed and delivered in the presence of us
David Gardener
Jeremiah Conkling

The Sachems
Sasogotacon
Checanor
Mauneehen

A similar second such conditional rental/conveyance was made by Wiandance on May 12, 1659 to one John Ogden,[24]

Be it knowne unto all men by this present writing that I Wiandance Sachem of Paumanwche on Long Island have upon deliberate consideration, and with my sonne Weeayacomboune, both of us together, given and granted unto Mr. John Ogden and his heirs for ever, I say freely given a certaine tract of land, beginning at the westward end of Southampton bounds, which land is bounded eastward by Southampton bounds, and with a small piece of meadow which I gave to Mr John Gosmer, which he is to enjoy, Northward to the water of the bay and to the creek of Accaboucke, Westward to the place called Pehecannache, and Southerly to Potuncke, three miles landward from the high water marke, and creek of accabouncke, and soe to the west,

But from this three miles breth of land southward all the land and meadows towards the south sea, the beach only excepted which I have sold to John Cooper, I say all the lands and meadows I have sold for a considerable price to Mr John Ogden for himself his heirs executors and assigns for ever upon conditions as followeth, first that Thomas Halsey and his associates shall have the privilege of the place of meadow called quaquanantuck, the term of years formerly granted to him or them, but the land lying betweene quaquanantuck and three miles, northward he shall or may posess and improve at present, but when the years of the aforesaid Thomas Halsey shall be expired, then shall the aforesaid Mr John Ogden or his assigns fully posess and improve all quaquanantuck meadow with the rest aforesaid, and then shall pay or cause to be paid unto me Wyandance my heirs and assigns the sum of twenty-five shillings a yeare as a yearly acknowledgement or rent for ever And it is also agreed that we shall keepe our privilege of fishing and fowling, or gathering berries of or any other thing for our use, and for the full and firme confirmation hereof we have both parties st too our hands markes and seals interchangeably...

Wiandance, as well as Gardner and Ogden, were careful in these conveyances, outright title was uncertain. Wiandance on the other hand looked out for the interests of the people whom he governed by the conditional stipulations contained in both deeds, that is, such important natural resources such as beached whales, bull rushes, fishing and fowling rights as well as herbage gathering rights. Both documents are a testament to the willingness of all parties involved to achieve an equitable agreement taking into consideration their respective needs. As we shall see later, these "western lands" were to become an issue involving the Shinnecock, the Town proprietors, individual title-holders, and the Governor General of the Province of New York.

III. Settling In

"the above named English shall defend us"

One of the foundations of the early relationship between the Town and the Shinnecock, and the Montauk for that matter, was the protection provided by the English against incursions by the Pequot, Narragansett, and Niantic tribes of Connecticut and Rhode Island. At the time of contact, the tribes of eastern Long Island were subordinate tributaries to the Pequot. Tradition held stories of raids, killings, and kidnappings by these tribes upon both the Montauk and Shinnecock. During the Pequot War, Wiandance and his Montauk warriors assisted the colonial forces against the Pequot. This assistance was indicative of the extent of the hostile feelings that the eastern Long Island Indians held towards the mainland Indians. In the aftermath of the Pequot War, the Narragansett and the Niantic under the sachem Ninigret attempted to take the place of their former Pequot liege. Wiandance forestalled their efforts. To prevent further strife Wiandance and the English agreed in the December 13, 1640 deed cited above that, "the above named English shall defend us the sayd Indians from the unjust violence of whatever Indians shall illegally assaile us…."

"several insolent injuries & insufferable outrages"

In an attempt to avoid any land conflicts with the Shinnecock, the Town Proprietors made it explicitly clear to the town inhabitants in a town ordinance dated October of 1642[1] that,

> Yt is ordered that noe man shall buy any land of the Indians with the bounds of this Towne without the consent of the Generall Court.

The Court here spoken of was Southampton's, given that Southampton had yet to join Connecticut Colony (1644). This law prevented the purchase of Indian title by individuals and limited such actions to committees of proprietors at the direction of the court.

By 1649, issues appeared between the Town and the Shinnecock. Complaints from townsmen appeared to the effect that the Shinnecock were planting on lands that were not theirs to do so. On the other hand, the Shinnecock complained to the proprietors concerning damages to their corn fields by wandering cattle and hogs belonging to certain townsmen. These townsmen, in turn, complained that their cattle were being injured by falling into corn pits dug by the Indians. To establish Shinnecock planting grounds on Shinnecock Plains, a continuing source of friction between the Shinnecock and the Town and to ensure the safety of the proprietors' cattle, a mutually satisfying agreement was concluded by the two parties on December 28, 1649.[2] A meeting[3] was held between the "Soaponack Indyans," the proprietors of Southampton, Wyandance, the Montauk sachem, and the noted Indian linguist Thomas Stanton, who acted both as interpreter and representative of the General Court of Connecticut Colony.

At this meeting they formulated "Articles of Agreem't" that settled the issue of which town-owned lands the Shinnecock were to use for planting:[4]

> At a Gen al Meeting of both the Townsmen of Southton aforesaid, and the said Indyans, of sabonack, It is fully now fully consented unto an -------- agreed upon beteweene the said Partyes, concerning the bounds of the sd Indyans, their lands as followeth; That the said Indyans are to have as their right and property, All the Planting Land lying westward from the head of Long Creek beyond the great Plain. Towards Shenecock, unto the Long Brook of Seponack aforesaid,

where Ware House belonging unto said English did formerly stand,...

As in circa 1640, the locus of Shinnecock settlement was to be found in Sebonnac ("Seponack").

The land allotted for Indian planting was firmly bounded and was to be enclosed by a fence. The Indians were to see to the safety of the Town's cattle by filling in unused corn pits. In return the Shinnecock allowed cattle grazing on their fields after the seasonal harvest, as well as to establish roads as needed.

Other problems were to come from different sources. In 1649 the wife of Thomas Halsey, one of the town proprietors, was murdered by an Indian, This created a concern of a general Indian uprising against the colonists. At first the Seponack Indians were suspected as the perpetrators of the act. Word was sent to Wiandance at his lodge at Montauk to come to Southampton. Wiandance was there with his friend Lion Gardner. Upon receipt of this summons concern was expressed for Wiandance's safety by his Indian associates, fearing that Wiandance might be held responsible for the murder. Gardner proposed that he remain at Montauk as a hostage, to ensure Wiandance's good treatment. Wiandance proceeded to Southampton. As Gardner recorded,[5]

> Soe when an English woman att or about Southampton was crewelly and Treacherously morthered by three Indians and one of the onely ones taken this Sagamore [Wiandance] seized the other two and himself bought them to justice at Hartford, wherein he gave good Testimoney of his fidelitie to the English and hazarded the love and Respect of his owne men whoe seldome heare of such a Currage in other Sagamores.

As it turned out, Mrs. Halsey's assailants turned out to be renegade Pequot, bent upon revenge against the colonists for their tribe's defeat.⁶ It was only through the combined efforts of Wiandance and Gardner that a conflict was averted between Southampton and the area Indians.

Further efforts were made to maintain peaceful relations with the Seponack or Shinnecock in 1651, when town laws were enacted to prevent overcharging Indians for bread, corn, and cloth, not to allow swine to wander upon Indian fields and to maintain fences to prevent such occurrences.⁷

In the aftermath of this issue two new ones arose. The first, in1653, was a renewed effort by the mainland Narragansett/ Niantic to politically dominate the Montauk and Shinnecock. An attempt was made by the Narragansett/Niantic sachem Ninigret to murder the sub-sachem of the Shinnecock, Mandush. The attempt failed, wherein the Narragansett attacked the Montauk in 1655, taking a number of them prisoner. At the same time reports surfaced indicating that the Dutch out of New Amsterdam were supplying the area's Indians with firearms,

> Captaine Topping and Jonas Wood in theire owne name and in the behalfe of Mr Fardom and Mr Ogden and others of South hamton by petition&c. enformed the Commissioners that theire peace is much endangered by that large trade the Indians have with the Duch in guns powder and shot by which meanes they are at least as plentifully furnished as themselves...but withal growne ensolent and Iniurius against the English....

These tensions culminated in 1657 with the burning of a number of houses in Southampton. The Town and the colony reacted in alarm. On May 15, 1657, Connecticut reacted with the following order,⁸

> Whereas the aforesaid Committee have received creible information of several insolent injuries & insufferable outrages committed against the inhabitants of South Hampton, by some Indians upon Long Island neare to said

South Hampton, but such as owne the Montacutt Sachem as their Sachem or Chiefe, they doe therefore hereby send you (as their agent, in behalf of this Colony) wth 19 men under command to South Hampton upon Long Island where you are to consider all matters & things whatsoever that may appeare necessary to bee considered and attended to yor ensuring instructions & you are to certify upon all occasions what shall bee theresult & issue of yor negotiations in refference to the prmises.

Wiandance, as the political leader of the Shinnecock was, under Connecticut law,[9] responsible for any crimes committed against any colonist or town by his wards. Upon his arrival with his contingent, Captain Mason undertook an investigation into the acts of arson. It was initially determined that three Shinnecock were involved. Based upon his findings, he levied a fine of 700 hundred pounds payable in seven years, against the Shinnecock. Wiandance as their leader was to be held responsible for the fine's payment.

It seems Mason rushed to judgment before all the facts of the matter were fully ascertained. Upon further investigation in Southampton, Wiandance petitioned the Commissioners of the United Colonies at Boston to reconsidered Mason's verdict and the fine levied upon him and his Shinnecock wards. The President of the Commissioners, Simon Bradstreet, wrote to his associates,

> …that by a misinformation or mistake in Reference to sume houses wilfully and sinfully burnt att Southhamton ptly by a wicked Indian who wee heare despartely killed himselfe to preuent Just execution; and ptly by a mischeuious Negar woman servant; fare deeper in that capitall miscarriage then any or all Indians; Major Mason Imployed in that service; not fully informed did lay a heavy penaltie upon then to pay 700 pound in seaven yeares, of the burden whereof they are now very sensable and desire ease…

The fine was reduced to 400 pounds by the Commissioners. Wiandance's payment of this fine was to play a major role in the westward expansion of Southampton's western boundary. The only asset held by the Shinnecock that was of value to the colonists was the remaining lands to which the Shinnecock still held aboriginal, or Indian title.

IV. The Western Lands

"quiet seizen and possession of all lands...."

As noted earlier, the only asset that the Shinnecock had with which to pay off the 400 pound fine was land. Those lands remaining to the Shinnecock were located west of the Canoe Carrying Place (Canoe Place, present-day Canoe Place Canal) extending westward to the Mastic River area near the Indian boundary between the Shinnecock and the neighboring Unkechaug Indians. At this time Wiandance and his son Weacomboune "Weeyacomboune" had entered into several leasehold agreements concerning certain tracts, including one of beach land and adjacent meadows to Lion Gardner mentioned earlier within this region.

On May 12, 1659 Wiandance and his son conveyed Indian title to a substantial tract land west of Canoe place to John Ogden with certain provisos,[1]

> A Certayne tract of land begining at ye westward end of Southampton bounds wch land is bounded eastward wth Southampton bounds and wth a small peece of meadow wch I gave to mr. John Gosmer wch he is to enjoy: Northward to the water of the bay and to the Creeke of Accabuck [Seponack' Shinnecok on Peconic Bay], Westward to the place called Peaconock[Peconic-Southampton-Riverhead] and Southerly to Potunck[Potunk-West Hampton], three miles Landward in from the hiewater marke and creeke of Accabocke an soe alPong the west...the beaeh only Excepted Wch is sould to John Cooper...for ever vpon Condition as ffolloweth ffirst that Thomas Halsey and his assosiates shall have the privilege of the place of meadow called Quaquanantuck the terme of yeares formerly grauted to him or them but the land lieinge betwene Quaquananantuck and

three miles northwards he shall or may possesse and improve at prsent, but when the yeares of the aforesd Thomas Halsey shallbe expired, then shall the aforesd Mr. John Ogden or his assignes fully possesse and improve all Quaquanantuck meadow...

Ogden was a town official, he was also a proprietor, and a town magistrate, as well one of the town's two representatives to the Connecticut General Court of Elections. His purchase of Indian title was not in the capacity of a private individual which would have been a violation of Connecticut colony law. The nature of this purchase was to obtain payment of the 400 pound fine, referred to as the "fire money." It was payment for the fine that encompassed lands from Canoe Place to Accabocke (Appacock) Creek in present-day Westhampton.

The nature of this conveyance was born out by a statement made by John Ogden in February of 1663[2] regarding his subsequent sale of these lands west of Canoe Place to the town attorney, John Scott. Scott in turn conveyed these lands to the town proprietors. Ogden's comments were as follows:

> Memerandum Mr John Ogden being present when the above deed was signed and sealed by John Scott Esq. hee the said Mr. John Ogden doth by subscribing owne that Wyandanch delivered unto him quiet seizen and possession of all lands above recited in part of pay of the four hundred pounds Shinecock Indiands stood indebted, and the said Wyandanck bound for the said Indians. As will more at large appeare in the said his Indians his and their heirs and assigns for ever...

At a Court session (Court of Session) held at Southold on June 7, 1665[3] the Court concurred that:

> Whereas Mr. Ogden did sell a parcell of Land to the Inhabitants of the towne of Southampton which was given and granted to him by ye late Sachem Wyandance & his son...

Three important facts are worth noting in regard to this conveyance to John Ogden. First, a clear legal conveyance of Shinnecocks' rights in vacant lands not belonging to any other town was made by Wiandance, the recognized political authority over the Shinnecock. Second, Ogden's obtained rights as grantee in these lands were subsequently conveyed to the Town of Southampton. Third, the conveyance to the Town was recognized by a Court having jurisdiction over the area. In 1667, John Ogden again confirmed that his rights to the lands west of Canoe Place had been conveyed to the Town of Southampton.[4]

It was indeed an unfortunate time for the Shinnecock. For the actions of one, all had to pay. It was representative of the times: suspicion, uncertainty, and perceived threats amounted to an overreaction, especially by Connecticut's Captain Mason and his apparently inept investigation. On the other hand Southampton was being threatened by the intrigues of the Niantic and Narragansett and the efforts by the Dutch to turn the eastern Long Island Indians against the English settlers.

Southampton had now gained the legal right to exclusive possession and occupancy of the lands west of Canoe Place from Peconic Bay to Shinnecock Bay, west to Accabocke Creek, just short of the present day boundary between the Towns of Southampton and Brookhaven. Although the Shinnecock ceded their Indian title to much of their lands west of Canoe Place, they could still hunt, harvest, and fish along its shores and inland waterways. Additionally the main Shinnecock village (Sebbonac) was to the east of Canoe Place and its principal wintering over village was near Accabocke Creek. The issue of these lands west of Canoe Place did not end here.

"all our right, title, and interest"

In 1655, the plantation of Seatuck (Sautaukett, later Brookhaven) was established with Indian title obtained to certain lands whose eastern boundary was upon the Mastic River (present day Forge River) from the Unkechauge Indians. The Unkechauge were also under the political domination of Wiandance. Seatuck was later to become the present day Town of Brookhaven. Like Southampton, Seatuk sought to come under Connecticut's jurisdiction. Permission was granted by Commissioners of the United Colonies in Boston in September of 1660,[5]

> Libertie is graunted to the Jurisdiction of Conecticott to take Huntington and Sautaukett two English Plantations on Long Iland into theire Gourment....

Likewise, Connecticut formally accepted the Town under her jurisdiction in May of 1661,[6]

> The Court understanding the Comrs consent thereunto, doe accept of ye Plantation of Setauk undr this Gouermt, upon ye same Articles of Confederation as are granted to Southampton; ...Mr Richard Wodhull and Mr. Thoms Peirce are chose by the Court to Officiate in ye place of Magistrates in the Plantat....

What is of importance here is that the boundaries of the 1659 John Ogden purchase from Wiandance extended from Canoe Place west to Accabocke Creek. This left the region between Accabocke Creek and Mastic River remaining under Indian title. At the same time (circa 1658), the Shinnecock, who generally occupied these western lands from Canoe Place to Seatuck Creek, lacked the political autonomy to control these lands. Wiandance was the sole title actuary.

On April 10, 1662, Thomas Topping, who like John Ogden was a Town magistrate as well as the second of the town's two representatives to the Connecticut General Court of Elections, purchased lands west of Canoe Place from Wiandance's spouse and political successor,[7] Weany Sunk Squaw:

> This writing made the tenth of April 1662 beteen Weany Sunk squaw, Anabackus and Iackanapes all of them residents of Shinecock near Southampton on Long Island, on the one partie and Thomas Topping of Southampton on the aforesaid Island on the other partie, Witnesseth that we the said Weany Anabackus and Iackakapes have given and granted and by these presents do give and grant bargain sell assign and set over unto Thomas Topping aforesaid his heirs and assigns for ever all our right title and interest that we have or ought to have in a certain tract of land lying and being westward of the said Shinnecock and the lawful bounds of Southampton above said, that is to say begin at canoe place otherwise Niamuck and soe to run westward to a place called and known by the name of Seatuck, and from thence to run northward across the said Island or neck of land unto a place called the head of the bay with all the meadow and pasture, arable land, easements profits benefits emoluments as is or may be contained within the limits or bounds before mentioned before mentioned together with half the profits and benefit, of the beach on the south side the said Island in respect of fish whale or whales that shall by God's providence be cast upon from time to time, and at all times, with all the herbage or beed that shall be, or grow thereon...

> In presence of

James Herrick	Thomas Topping
John Topping	Weany
Elnathan Topping	Anabackus
	Iackanapes
	Cobish
	Topobin
	Wetaugon

In this instrument of conveyance, Wyandance's political successor, "Weany Suncks Squaw conveyed "all our right, title, and interest" to Thomas Topping. "Weany Sunk" (Sunk

Squaw) (1662) was variously described in some primary and secondary sources as Wiandance's widow, sister, or daughter. The preponderance of primary source records described her as his spouse.[8] She assumed this position after the death of Wiandance's only son Wiacombe. Such an assumption by the "Sunck Squaw" (literally woman leader) was not uncommon amongst the region's Indians, especially in southern New England.

Although this land, as in the Ogden purchase, was not part of any town or colony grant, Southampton asserted her special rights given to her by the Connecticut General Court back in 1643,

> the said Towne shal have liberite to regulate themselues according as may be most sutable to theire own comforts and conueniences in theire own judgment, provided those orders made by them concerne themselues only and intrence not upon ye interests of others of ye Generall Combination of ye united Collonies, and not cross to ye rule of riteousness. The like power is also reserved unto themselves for the future, for making of such orders as may concerne theire Town ocations....

As indicated above, Southampton, by virtue of her special relationship with Connecticut, again expanded her western boundary into lands not held by any other town.

What Topping did was to repurchase the lands of the Ogden Purchase as well as the remaining Shinnecock lands between Canoe Place (Niamuck) and Accabocke Creek from Weany Sunk. This extended Southampton's western boundary to the eastern boundary of Seatuck. Under this conveyance the Shinnecock retained,

> ...half the profits and benefit, of the beach on the south side the said Island in respect of fish whale or whales that shall by God's providence be cast upon from time to time, and at all

times, with all the herbage or beed that shall be, or grow thereon....

This conveyance document made no mention of Indian exclusion from, or use of, this newly acquired territory. During this time period the main Shinnecock village and agricultural fields remained in the northern section of the Shinnecock Hills area of Southampton, adjoining Peconic Bay. It was called Sebonnac. Archaeological research confirms that this site, in the vicinity of the present-day Shinnecock Hills Country Club, was occupied by the Shinnecock by 1602[9] and remained so until around 1860.

Additionally, the conveyance stated that the southern seashore resources (Atlantic Ocean) remained equally available to both Southampton and the Shinnecock. Despite this, two controversies were to emerge from this conveyance. One was with Thomas Topping the other, with the Shinnecock.

As noted earlier, this conveyance was performed whilst Southampton was still part of the colony of Connecticut. The land so purchased by Topping was for lands unclaimed by any other town and not in the formal possession of another English colony or province. Royal confirmation of Connecticut's long-standing claim to the lands of Long Island was not formalized by King James II until April 20, 1662,[10] that is, ten days after the Topping Purchase conveyance instrument was signed. These lands so purchased belonged to no other town or colony. The Dutch claimed all of Long Island, a fact that was not recognized by the English Crown.

Once the lands of Long Island formally became part of Connecticut via the King's signature to Connecticut's royal charter, Topping, acting in his dual capacity as a town magistrate and colony official, was required by Connecticut law to either convey the lands he purchased to Southampton or to the colony.[11] Weany Sunk conveyed the Indian title to these lands to Topping, not the Town. Topping, as did Ogden, had to convey his acquired right to the Town in order for Southampton to take possession of the lands at issue. The problem that emerged was that Topping and the Town could not come to an agreement as to what constituted fair compensation for his efforts and costs in obtaining the conveyance of these lands west of Canoe Place. Thomas Topping refused to relinquish his right until the Town proprietors agreed to his compensation demands.

This stalemate continued on for two years during which time jurisdiction over Long Island was transferred by King James II from Connecticut to his brother, the Duke of York.[12] Richard Nicolls, the Duke's trusted assistant and longtime confidant, became Governor General of the newly acquired Province of New York. It was on December 1, 1664, that Governor Nicolls notified Southampton that it was now subject to the Province of New York.

During this period of political transition, the issue between Topping and the Town remained unresolved. Thus the entire matter was put before Governor Nicolls to adjudge.[13] He rendered his decision on the matter to the Town:

> Whereas Mr. John Howell, and Mr Henry Pierson are deputed by the town of Southampton to proscecute or conclude a difference with Capt Thomas Topping, which difference hath also a relation to John Cooper in respect of his claime of Interest, to which end all ye said parties shewed several writings whereof were three deeds, one of these from John Scott to Southampton men, another from Lyon Gardiner to John Cooper, Now know all persons by these presents that ye said parties namely Capt. Thomas Topping, the said deputies from Southampton and John Cooper, have fully and absolutely reffered themselves to my determination in the premises whereupon(with ye consent of ye said parties) I doe conclude and determine as followeth, yt they the said Capt

Thomas Topping and John Cooper shall fully and freely (upon demand) deliver unto the town of Southampton all their deeds, writing and evidences that they have of a certain tract of land now in contraversie between them, and which the said towne purchased of John Scott as by his deed aforesaid, appeareth, and all the right and interest that ye said Capt Thomas Topping and John Cooper have by the said deeds or any other way or means obtained, in the said tract of land meadows or beach mentioned in their said deeds is belonging, doth and shall belong unto the town of Southampton (viz) (that have and doe pay purchase), and their successors forever, herein only profits of whales excepted, and they the said Capt. Thomas Topping and John Cooper and either of them shall hereafter sign any instrument in writing that may be made for ye further confirmation of their said interest unto the said Southampton, And in consideration whereof the towne of Southampton shall pay to him ye said Capt. Thomas Topping or his assigns the sum of five pounds, and they shall alsoe pay unto ye Indians (concerned to receive it) four score fathoms of wampum, the wampum being accompted at six per penny, or soe much in value in pay equivalent, the same to be distributed to all the Indians (according to ye interesr they had In ye premises purchased) at ye best discretion of Mr John Howell Henry Pierson and Richard Howell, Also the said towne shall let him the said Capt. Topping have 150L allotment ye said meadows…all which is in consideration of the interest which he the said Capt Topping claimeth in the whales, which may be cast upon the beach within the compass of the forementioned purchase and designed as above written the which interest in all the profits of whales & fish shall belong unto him the said John Cooper his heirs and assigns for ever, and hee the said Capt. Topping shall at any time hereafter upon Reasonable demand signe any deed or writing that is or shall be made further to confirm unto the said John Cooper his heirs and assigns the said interest in whales or fish &c and he the said John Cooper in content to accept in what ye town of Southampton shall freely pay unto him for the herbage of the beach which he hath resigned up unto the said town as afore said, and this to be the ultimate issue and final determination concerning the premises and I doe alsoe confirme and assure unto the said town there said tract of land with the said herbage of the beach &c, and to ye said John Cooper his said Interest in the profits of whales or fish, and defend them and their in peaceable enjoyment thereof Against all other claims whatsoever.

Dated in Fort James in New York the 3rd day of October 1666

Richard Nicolls

The important point is that the issue of the conveyance of western lands was not the central subject of the Governor's determination, nor was the Shinnecock directly involved in this specific matter. The main focus was to arrive at a decision whereby just compensation would, on the basis of the arguments presented to the Governor, be made to Thomas Topping regarding the Shinnecock land acquisition so that the land's title could be passed to Southampton. In a separate issue, Governor Nicolls directed that the Shinnecock be given compensation for their conveyance of the lands west of Canoe Place. In his determination, he did not question the validity of Topping's purchase, Nicolls' only role was that of an arbiter.

In his determination, Governor Nicolls directed that the Town receive full standing as feeholder of the lands west of Canoe Place. The Governor did not question the legality of the Shinnecock conveyance of their rights to the lands west of Canoe Place to Topping. By virtue of this determination, Governor Nicolls acknowledged the validity of Topping's purchase and quieted the remaining Shinnecock claims to the area. Topping received his fair compensation, the Shinnecock did also. The Town of Southampton acquired a clear title and the exclusive right of occupancy to all these western lands:

> The Governor was pleased to declare that hee did ye last yeare about the Matter in Controversy betweene Capn

Tapping and ye Towne of Southampton which was then composed, Hoe only Confirmed the right that either of them really had, but did not create any new Right in either of them.

Nicolls did not issue an order imposing a settlement between Topping and the Town. Following his past practice, he was advised, he listened, and he forged a peaceful equitable resolution. The Shinnecock played but a minor part in the proceedings. On November 6, 1667,[14] Thomas Topping conveyed his right to the lands west of Niamuck (Canoe Place) to the Town of Southampton. The lands between Canoe Place and Seatuck, including Westwoods, now belonged to Southampton.

Additionally, Weany Sunk, together with the Shinnecock confirmed the conveyance via a February 22, 1666 affirmation document:[15]

> Whereas some of us the under named Indians of Shinnecock, namely Weany, Accobacco, and others, did sell unto Capt. Thomas Topping a certaine tract of land and meadows and appeareth by a deed bearing date the 10th of April, 1662, and hee having assigned the said deed and land unto Southton men of New Yorkshire and hee being to pay for the said purchase fourscore fathom of wampum at six penny or equivalent thereunto. And the honorable Governor Nichols having appointed the sais Southton men to pay the wampum as by a writing under his hand, now know all man by these presents, that we the subscribed of the said Shenecock Indians doe avouth the said tract of land sold at the above said with all the appurtenances thereto belonging and priviledges therof to bee our owne property Interests and right to sell and dispose of and wee are fully contented with the bargaine originally made with Capt. Topping as aforesaid and with his assignment of the premises unto Southton men. And wee acknowledge to have received from them by the hands of Mr. John Howell. Henry Pierson, and Richard Howell (appointed by the Governor Nicolls to deliver it) the full sum of fourscore fathom of good wampum and alsoe a gratuity

from Southton men of theire own voluntary good wills they give us whereby wee take ourselves fully satisfied for the said tract of land, meadows, creekes within the limits mentioned in the said deed unto Capt. Topping reaching to the head of North Bay and so running to the South beach to the place appointed by the said deed which is all the land and meadows thence Eastward betweene the South Sea and the Bay called Peconnet unto the Cannoue place alias Niamuck And nce will uphold and warrentize the said land and privileges unto the Southton men their heyres and successor To have and to hold the same without any molessacon by us or any in our names and wee will defend the Southton men in the possession and enjoyment of the premises from the claym of any other: witness our hands this 22th of February 1666.

In the aftermath of the Governor's Determination, on September 17, 1666, a dissident group of Shinnecock made claim that Weany Sunk did not have the right to initially convey the lands purchased by Topping.[16] They asked the Governor for compensation as a means of settling the dispute:

…And wee the true proprietors of the said lands, doe hereby assigne and make ouer, all our said Interest in the said tract of land, lying from a place called Niamuck or ye canoe place, westward to a place called Seatuck, and soe to run cross ye Island (namely Long Island) unto a place called the head of the bay, or Peaconnet, on the north, wee say wee doe impart and assigne all our interest in ye said lands, (whereof Qwagwanantuck is part) unto our ancient and loving ffriends the Townes men of Southampton to them and their successors for ever, with this proviso & consideration that if General Nicolls whom wee acknowledge the hon & discreet Governor of this Island doth upon examination finde us or part of us to bee the true proprietors of ye said lands before mentioned.

"the said persons or Indians had noe right"

This 1666 petition marks a significant turning point in the Shinnecock's political history. The Shinnecock residing at

Sebbonack had apparently fissioned off into two competing political factions. First, there were the traditionalists who recognized Weany Sunk as the legitimate political successor to her husband and son and her leadership. Second, there was what may be termed the independence faction who no longer recognized Weany Sunk's leadership legitimacy and by extension those of the Montauk Indians over the Shinnecock people. In their eyes, Shinnecock lands were conveyed by Montauk overlords. Another hallmark here was the direct petition to the governor by this faction rather than attempting to resolve the issue with the town proprietors.

The February 22, 1666 Shinnecock affirmation[17] of the Topping purchase provides a roll of Weany's followers who acknowledged their support of her conveyance to Topping.

> ...The markes of chachasy Nowidatasoni Apabackabang Micksan Cageponas his wives marke being Mandush sister Cagepanas Cobish wife her marke the Relic of Mandush Augumneed Chanaquam Chanaquam Octaives Amagish Weany a woman Quaquashaw Accohacco Jhaskhanso Tyabbin John Man Moncatomo Mantuomuh Pungumo Judas Apunch Samwason Mamnum

Seven months later, political fissioning had occurred amongst the Shinnecock. On September 17, 1666, a faction of Shinnecock protested the conveyance to Topping, arguing the fact that neither Weany Sunk nor those other signatories to the conveyance had the right to do so. Several of the dissident signatories were also attestors to the February 22, 1666 affirmation document,[18]

> Know all men by these presents, that whereas wee the underwritten whoe are of the Indians of Shinecock, and understanding that some of our Indians have namely Weany, Annobaccus, Iackanapes & some others have sold unto Capt Topping a tract of land westward from Southampton bounds, wee, doe hereby make protest against the said sale, and doe

affirme yt the said persons or Indians had noe right to make any such sale, but that ye interest and propriety unto the said land belongeth totally or principally unto us or some of us And wee the true proprietors of the said lands, doe hereby assigne and make ouer, all our said Interest in the said tract of land, lying from a place called Niamuck or ye canoe place, westward to a place called Seatuck, and soe to run cross ye Island (namely Long Island) unto a place called the head of the bay, or Peaconnet, on the north, wee say wee doe impart and assigne all our interest in ye said lands, (whereof Qwagwanantuck is part) unto our ancient and loving ffriends the Townes men of Southampton to them and their successors for ever, with this proviso & consideration that if General Nicolls whom wee acknowledge the hon & discreet Governor of this Island doth upon examination finde us or part of us to bee the true proprietors of ye said lands before mentioned, And that the said Southampton men doe receive and pocess the same upon our right or accompt, that then they shall pay unto us, as is said honor shall determine.

Witness our hands this 17th of September, 1666

Mandush his daughter
Quaquashaw
Anoineis Punch Mandush his sonne
Weetetosen
Ionaquid
Goabes wife the relic of Mandush the chief Sachem
Sawgum
Hoaquemes
Apuckhowbatk
Somwesesen
John Smith

What is especially significant concerning the signatories of this document is the presence of the marks of the wife, daughter, and son of Mandush. Mandush, it will be recalled, participated in the 1648 "Cowaunckamish" ritual that was witnessed by Thomas Halsey by which Mandush acknowledged Wiandance's right and authority over the

Shinnecock and their lands. Now Mandush's heirs and sympathizers were attempting to throw off the yoke of Montauk political domination. That same year, Governor Lovelace essentially left the issue of Indian affairs on Long Island up to commissioners appointed by the towns located there. Lovelace ordered,[19]

> ...You are hereby Authorized to make such Orders and Constitutions, as you shall finde necessary and expedient for the better regulating all matters and Affaires between the English and Indyans of yor parts aforesaid, of which you are to give one Copy to ye Indyans, and remitt another to mee for Confirmation....

V. "being destitute of such a person"

In the aftermath of Governor Nicolls' arbitration of the Topping and Shinnecock issues, there remained, due to internal factionalization, no specifically recognized Shinnecock leader who could speak for all the Shinnecock people to the town and provincial authorities. If the Shinnecock at Sebbonack were to survive as a community and to have their voice heard by those who could affect their survival, a resolution to the Shinnecock's political diverseness had to be effected. Such a resolution was not to be forthcoming from within the tribe. In 1670, the provincial government, led by Governor Francis Lovelace, took the necessary steps to create political unity amongst the Shinnecock. On January 2, 1670, the Governor issued the following commission[1] to the Shinnecock community,

A Commission for ye Indian named
Quaquashawg to be Sachem.
Francis Lovelace, Governor of the Province of New York.

Francis Lovelace Esqr &c. Whereas It hath beene usuall & is found very convenient that some Person amongst ye Indians should in theire respective Tribes or Nations be as cheife or Sachem over ye rest as well to keep them in ye bettr order as to be responsible for any mischeife they should happen to comitt, & ye Indians neare Southampton in ye East Ryding of Yorkshire upon Long Island commonly called ye *Shinnacock* Indians *being destitute of such a person* having nominated & elected *Quaquashawge* to be theire Sachem who is likewise approved of by ye English to be a fitt person amongst them for that purpose by reason of his quiet and peaceable disposition, I have thoughr fitt to confirme & appoint ye said Indian *Quaquashawg to be Sachem over ye Shinnecock Indians* of ye wch they are all to take notice & obey him as theire cheife and Sachem (emphasis added).

The New York provincial government took the step of insisting that the Shinnecock choose a single leader, a "cheife or Sachem" to assume responsibility for all the Shinnecock as did Wiandance and Weany Sunk. This time, such leadership was to be of their own choosing. It was by Governor Lovelace's action that the Shinnecock did, for the first time historically, unite under one recognized political leader. One of the significant acts made by Governor Nicolls in 1670 was to banish the position of superior sachems, such as Wiandance, over all the Indian groups on Long Island. The Shinnecocks could finally be politically autonomous, free of Montauk dominance. Their choice of sachem was subject to the approval of the governor. "Quaquashawg," the Shinnecock's choice was a signatory to both the February 1666 affirmation of the Topping purchase as well as one of the factional signatories to the September petition opposing Weany Sunk's authority. The Shinnecock, by acceding to the Governor's authority in this matter, acknowledged the province's legal jurisdiction over them and their affairs.

The following year the province also mandated further political changes in the way the Shinnecock were governed. This time the province imposed the position and authority of constable upon the Shinnecock. Such a constable, as was his town counterpart, was required to see that provincial law was followed and to apprehend transgressors. On January 4, 1671,[2] a Shinnecock named "Cawbutt" was commissioned by the province to fulfill that position,

> A Commission for an Indian Constable
> amongst ye Shinnacock Indians.
>
> Whereas it has beene proposed unto me that for ye bettr keeping of ye Indians in good order it would be requisite that one amongst them should be nominated and appointed as Constable, & that he may have a staffe wth ye Kings Armes

thereon by ye Reputation whereof ye rest of ye Indians may be kept in a more quiet & peaceable condicon And having beene sued to for a Confirmation of a Sachem over ye Indians neare Southampton commonly called ye Shinnacock Indians ye wch accordingly I have graunted I do hereby allow of ye Indian called *Cawbutt* who is recommended to be a person of peaceable temper to be Constable amongst ye said Shinnacock Indians, & that he have a Constable Saffe as is desired. He is by vurtue of his office to keep his fellow Indians in good order, & to suffer no violence or abuses to be offer'd amongst them by Ecesse of Drinke or otherwise, & withal to obey his Sachem & to observe ye Rules & orders appointed by ye Comrs for ye Indian affaires there for ye doing Whereof this shall be his warrant. Given under my hand at ffort James in New York this 4th day of January in ye 22th yeare of his Maties Raigne Ano Dm 1671.

What is especially telling here was that Cawbutt was to be presented with a constable's staff as a sign that he was a provincial official, not a tribal official. His powers, as signified by the seal affixed on the staff, were no different from any other person holding this office either in the New World or in England. Oddly, Cawbutt, a provincial officer, was vested with greater political power than did the Shinnecock's sachem, Quaquashawg.

Within three years Quaquashawg was replaced as sachem of the Shinnecock by Anabacus. The Southampton town records note this change wherein Quaquashawg appears as a councilor after Anabacus who was identified as "the sachem." Anabacus was a supporter of Weany Sunk as a signatory to both the April 1662 Topping purchase deed and the February 1666 Topping affirmation statement. In this town record entry,[3] dated May 2, 1672, the Shinnecock leadership was being summoned by the town's Justice of the Peace, Thomas Delavall to meet with town officials to "mutally" settle differences between the town and the Shinnecock,

Shenecock Indians being summoned to make their appearance before Major Thomas Delavall this day for the settling some matters of Difference concerning the Towne and the sd Indians, They the said Indians, or a great part of the chief of them, as the sachem *Anabaccus Quaquashang Upponeh Johnman Anagwanack, Ionaquit*, And many others being assembled together with the constables and overseers, and divers of the neighbors of the said towne...doe determine and mutally agree as followeth...The Major is content for this time, But engageth ye Constable of this town to look diligently to his office and see that the Indians keep good order, And if any of them for time future shall offend in like nature as to breake windows, affright women, or offer violence to any, they are to be severely punished or sent up to N. Yorke....

It is apparent that both sides were seeking a solution to prevent further mischievous acts purportedly being instigated by Indians under Anabacus' jurisdiction.

Fourteen years later, Pungamo, the son of Mandush (circa 1648), the Shinnecock sub-sachem under Wiandance, was the Shinnecock's singular leader. A November 24, 1686 affirmation[4] of the original December 1640 purchase of the original lands of Southampton depicted this change. This affirmation was needed by the town in order to receive a formal patent or confirmation of Southampton's lands from Governor Thomas Dongan. Such patents issued in the King's name confirmed that the town of Southampton held a clear, fee simple title to all the lands within its boundaries that were in no way subject to any Indian or aboriginal title rights or claims. The affirmation document stated,

> This day appeared before me Llift. Collonll John Youngs, Esq. one of his Majesties Justicicces of the peace, eleven of the Chiefs of the Indians of Shinecock, namely: Pungamo, Sachem who is son and heire to the within subscribed Mandush, and quaquashawg, John man, Cobil, asport, palamcowet, wahambahaw, wiackhance, Suretrust, Saspan,

Ahickock, five whereof being old men, did declare before me as followeth (viz) that the aforesaid Mandush, sachem and true proprietor with these Indians with him subscribed to ye written deed, with ye full consent of the rest of the Indians of Shinecock & did according to this deed as within written sell and alienate the said lands to the English therein named and did alsoe declare that upon theire that upon theire certaine knowledge they knew that within said payment for the said lands was by the said English made to the said Indians according to covenant as within expressed, to theire content, and that all the forenamed Indians did this day unamimously acknowledge and consent unto the written Deed according to the true uintent thereof as atest my hand the day and year aforesaid.

John Youngs.

In this situation, it was the Shinnecock who aided the town of Southampton in validating the authenticity, and thus the legality, of its founding documents.

In the aftermath of the 1662 Topping purchase and the subsequent issues that devolved from it, the Shinnecock, as a people, were at a crossroads whether they were to survive as both a social and cultural entity. It was by the actions or non-actions of both the provincial government and the town that provided key enabling factors that allowed for this community's continued existence.

The New York provincial government did, via its actions in eliminating so-called "super sachems," force an end to the political factionalism within the community, and by requiring the community to unify under a single sachem, politically unify the Shinnecock. Additionally, by having a direct representative of the government, in the form of an Indian constable to maintain peace within the community, who worked to maintain a social equilibrium and environment within the community, the government prevented large-scale out-migrations of Shinnecock as many Montauk did later to

Indian new polyglot communities amongst the Iroquois of upper New York.

At the same time, the town aided this equilibrium by allowing the increasingly ethnically isolated Shinnecock community to remain upon its traditional lands at Sebbonac, and to maintain its traditional subsistence activities within the town's newly acquired western lands. Access to these lands was important for subsistence activities such as hunting and fishing. Additionally, the Shinnecock's wintering- over village site at Quag was near the seashore in the vicinity of Appacock Creek. Other important factors played key roles. The lack of warfare between the colonists and the Shinnecock wherein there was no ideologically depressed defeated people as a result, and the willingness to mutually work through their differences rather than resort to outright political dominance to settle such issues helped to maintain stability within the community. Additionally, the Shinnecock community became isolated from the Montauk Indians due to land cessions to Southampton and similar Montauk cessions to Easthampton as well as Unkechauge land cessions to Mastic/Brookhaven. As a result, social and ethnic boundaries contracted, with primary identification being with the local Sebonnac village community and its leadership. Within this matrix a localized identity of being "Shinnecock" was born.

Was this willingness by the Shinnecock and the town to accommodate, and adapt to one another to continue?

VI. The Thousand Year Lease

"by and with the consent of our people"

By the end of the seventeenth century a sizable Shinnecock population remained. A census[1] conducted in 1698 reported a total Shinnecock population of 152 persons of whom fifty-two were above fifteen years of age. One hundred of these people were women and children. By 1703, the Shinnecock had also adjusted their political structure from one sachem to three, "Pungamo, Gice, Mamanamon." By this action the Shinnecock hoped to avoid the pitfalls of a one man representative to the outside world. It might also be representative of political factionalism within the community. It appears in documents, to be addressed below, that unanimity amongst the three was required for an action to occur. Additionally, it appears that these three governed by the consent of those who they represented. A major Shinnecock concern was the maintenance of a land base for their people. Southampton's non-Indian population was growing and the town's settlement footprint was expanding. Such concerns were the subject of a meeting on August 13, 1703, that the three sachems had with Southampton's proprietary trustees. On the day previous, the three had met with the town to again reaffirm all the previous deeds between the Shinnecock and the Town. Of interest we note for the first time that the three Shinnecock sachems, "Pungamo, Gice, Mamanamon," reaffirmed these conveyances "by and with the consent of our people and in the behalfe as well as for ourselves"[2] The three carried out their responsibilities with the consent of the community. This was a far cry from the days of Yovawan, Wiandance, and Weany Sunk.

As noted earlier, the August 13, 1703[3] meeting with the town trustees concerned "some dissatisfaction" over land. The two parties debated the issue and agreed to meet again on August 16 to formally fix the town boundaries,[4] which they did,

> wherewith ye said *Pomquamo, Chice,* and *Mahanaman* Indian sachems above sd acknowledge themselves ffully satisfied contented and paid, hath given granted remised released and forever quit claim unto ye said trustees namely Elnathan Topping, Joseph Ffordham, Joseph Peirson, Abraham Howell, Jeckamiah Scott, Josiah Howell, Daniel Halsey, Thomas Stephens, Joseph Howell, Gershum Culver, John Malbie, and Hezekiah Howell of ye commonality of ye town of Southampton and their associates their heirs sucksesors forever, in their full and peasible possession and seaseing, for all such right, estate, title, interest and demand whatsoever, as they ye said *Pomgomo, Chice* and *Mahanaman* and their people had or out to have of in or to all that tracte of land of ye township of Southampton...

Besides the three sachems as subscribers to the Act, other Shinnecock were co-subscribers to the deed,

> Tomon, Issac, Obadiah, Ned, Wegan, Wackwanna, Judas, Benquam, Nahanawas, Toby, Achigan, Longatuck, Quatagaboge

In return for their confirmation of Southampton's lands, the Shinnecock received what they needed most, land, in the form of a 1,000 year conditional usufructory lease,[5]

> This indenture made between the Trustees of the commonality of the town of Southampton of Suffolk and province of New York on the island of Nassau on the one part, and *Pomquama, Chice,* and *Manaman* and their people belonging to the Shinnecock of the other part, witnesseth, : That the said trustees of the town aforesaid, by and with one full consent and agreement for divers good, causes them thereunto moving, and one ear of Indian corn annually to be

paid to the Trustees of said Town from the time being, yearly, and every year, upon the first day of November, and for and upon the condition and proviso here after expressed have demised, granted, and to farm letten, and by these presents do demise, grant, let, and let to farm unto the said *Pomquama, Chice, Manaman*, and their people abovesaid, all that certain tract of land lying within the bounds of Southampton aforesaid, called by the name of *Shinnecock* and *Sebonac*, bounded west by Canoe place, alias *Niamug*, and bounded southward by Shinnecock Bay, and eastward by a line running from the head of Shinnecock Creek to the north-west corner of James Cooper's Close, and from thence northwardly to the westward part of Jonathan Raynor's land, at Sebonac old ground, and from thence on a direct line to a place called the warehouse by the North Bay, and on the north by the said Bay; meadows, marshes, grass, herbage, feeding and pasture, timber, stone, and convienent highways only excepted, with all and singular the privileges and advantages of plowing and planting, and timber for firing and fencing, and other conveniences and benefits whatsoever, excepting what before was excepted to the only use and behoof of the said Indians, their heirs and successors, for one thousand years thence next ensuring the date thereof: Provided always the said Indians do not keep nor cause to be kept, any part or parcel of the said land within fence or enclosed from the last of October to the first of April, from year to year, during the whole term aforesaid; and for the full confirmation hereof, the parties have interchangeably set their hands and seals in Southampton aforesaid, this sixteenth of August, Anno Dom 1703...

We, the trustees within named, according to the Town's former agreement with the said Indians of Shinnecock do hereby grant liberty to them and theirs, to cut flags, bulrushes, and such grass as they usually make their mats and houses of, and to dig ground nuts, mowing lands excepted anywhere in the bounds of Southampton aforesaid, as witnessed our hands and seals this 16th day of August, 1703.

The Shinnecock gained what amounted to perpetual usufructory rights to the lands within "Shinnecock and Sebonac" for residing and agricultural use as well as flags, bulrushes, and grass. They were also allowed to harvest timber "for firing and fencing" as well as hunting and fishing. As specified above, the town reserved a share of natural resources for its own use, "meadows, marshes, grass, herbage, feeding and pasture, timber, stone." The town also reserved the right of roadways through the region. In recognition of the town's continued ownership of the lands, the Shinnecock were required to make an annual symbolic fealty payment to the trustees of one ear of corn. Most important was the fact that the town had guaranteed the Shinnecock continued residence within the town and the continued use of their traditional lands. This act makes it clear that the town was not intent on destroying the Shinnecock community or driving them out. If that had been the case all the town trustees would have only had to expel them from Sebonac and prohibit their use of the lands west of Canoe Place.

VII. Transformation 1703-1860

Accommodations

In the aftermath of the 1703 lease agreement there were limited recorded contacts between the town trustees and proprietors and the Shinnecock residing within the leased lands through 1790. In fact, there appeared to be no discernable political authority within the tribe that was capable of effectively regulating the actions of tribal members. Azaiah Horton, the Presbyterian Missionary, reflected upon the fact (circa 1743) that his efforts among both the Montauk and Shinnecock were being impeded, "partly by Reason Divisions and Confusions are among the Inhabitants of the adjacent places."[1]

Except for two petitions (1764, 1782) presented to the town, and two actions by the town trustees concerning leases of woodlots (1744, 1747) there are no documented contacts between identified tribal leaders or groups of individuals representing the Shinnecock community at large or any Town officials during this 87 year period.[2] These were quiet times of co-existence.

By virtue of the 1676 Dongan Patent, the "trustees of the ffreeholders and commonalty of the Towne of Southampton" had the authority to regulate the "common privileges" within Southampton. Among these "privileges" was the right to manage the town's natural resources including timber on undivided town common lands and waterways. Additionally, the town trustees had the authority to lease out common lands or the resources in or upon them to individuals or groups.[3]

During this period (1741-1790), there were many town trustee meetings at which actions affecting the Shinnecock's leased lands were recommended, voted upon, and put into effect by the town trustees. These actions included the maintenance of natural resources within the leased lands and protecting the Shinnecock's lands. Town records failed to disclose the presence of any Shinnecock at any of these meetings.

On a yearly basis Southampton elected officials to manage lands within the town,

> At a town meeting april ye 1 1746 of the free holders of Southampton according to ye Tenure of our Pattent to elect and chuse Town officers for this Insuring year, and ye sd free holders do proseed to their choyce as followeth, ...Town Clerk... Constable... Supervisors of Intestate estates, assessor... Collector... trustee [9]... viewers of fences... commissioners...

At the same meeting the town took steps to protect the Shinnecock lands within the leased area,

> ...It is voted that no man shall plow or plant any corn in ye Indian land except ye Indians themselves upon ye penalty of twenty shillings an acre....[4]

This admonition and the threat of penalty appeared repeatedly in the Town trustee records during this time period. As noted in the following records, the Town took care to protect those lands within the leased lands that the Shinnecock were utilizing. The records also noted the prosecution of violators,

> Also ordered and Enacted by said Trustees that Absolom Cooper Esq. and Isaac Post are hereby appoinnted authorised and impowered to sur Jonas Foster in an action of trepas for his planting of corn & soing of oats at Shenacok on the Indian land and that b upon the Coust of the Town.[5]

> May, 22 1751 Shenecock Pounders.- Allso Voted and ordered at the same meeting that Abram Cooper Esq'r and Jonas foster shall be & Hereby are authorized and impowered to

impound all such Creatures as they Shall finde trespas in the Indian fields where they plant corn.

April 3, 1750…at a town meeting it is voted that no person shall so any flax or ots or any other grain on the Indian land upon the penalty of forty shillings per acre…[6]

At a meeting of the Trustees…at the Schoolhouse.. It was then and there ordered that Thomas jennings and Joseph Foster shall be Pounders for the Indians….

April 6, 1762
Also ordered by sd Trustees ther shall not be any flax sead or oats soed on any part of the Indian land on penalty of twenty Shilling pr/acre for every acre & so in proportion for any quantity so soed contrarary to the true intent of this Act…[7]

July 22, 1785
…And there is full power given to Samuel Cooper David Rose Moses Rose to prosecute all such all such persons as do leave the gates open belonging to the Inden field Also to see that the Indens have a sufficient fence.[8]

During this period, the town trustees records also noted the opening and closing of lands within the leased areas for conservation purposes. Shinnecock Neck was seasonally closed to grazing and fences there maintained by committees appointed by the trustees. Beach gathering of seaweed was also regulated (sunrise to sunset). Pounders continually watched over the leased lands for loose horses, sheep, and cattle that could upset the ecology of the lands and damage the Shinnecock's crops.[9] Timber harvesting was closely monitored. In other words, the natural resource "exceptions" cited in the 1703 lease were utilized by, and closely husbanded, by the town. In other words, the town carefully maintained the natural resources within the town's boundaries, including those within the Shinnecock leased area.

"the wood will soon be done"

As the town population grew both in numbers and economically, both the town and the Shinnecock faced the specter of dwindling timber resources. John Lyon Gardiner, writing in July of 1798, noted: "the wood will soon be done unless it is preserved by Legislative authority."[10] The noted theologian Timothy Dwight, also observed the effects of eventual deforestation in Southampton in 1804. Dwight described the 1703 leased lands between Southampton township and Canoe Place in the following manner,[11]

> From Southampton to what is here called the Canoe Place, about four miles, the country is a succession of disagreeable sand hills, a considerable part of which is blown, like the grounds formerly mentioned in the description of Cape Cod, and exhibit a desolate and melancholy aspect. These hills were once cultivated, but from the poverty of the soil and the ravages of the wind appear to have been finally forsaken...

Readily accessible and sufficient timber lands were probably the most important natural resource to either a colonial or sedentary Indian community after that of potable water and the presence of arable lands for agricultural use.

Yet, within one hundred years of the founding of Southampton, the town records demonstrate a growing concern for the over harvesting of timber land within the town's boundaries. At the same time the town trustees sought to protect those timber lands being utilized by the Shinnecock,

> Southampton May ye 5th 1741 Ordered by the Trustees that noe timber shall be cutt nor carted in Shinecock great neck this year and any that shall cutt wood thire shall pay six shillings a load to be recovered by any Justice, a pice.[12]

> April 2, 1745...Voted on sd day at the above sd meting that there shall not be any timber Cut or Carted in Shenecock Great Neck on penality of Six Shillings per Load for every

Load so Cutt or carted away Contrary to true intent and meaning of the act and als there shall be no timber Cut or Carted in Sebonock Great Neck on penalty of Six Shillings pr. Load for every load so cut or carted as above sd.[13]

While imposing these restrictions, the town was also mindful of the rights to timber accorded to the Shinnecock,

> April 1, 1746, ...and orded-By said Trustees yt No man shall Cutt nor Cart any Timber In Shinecock or Sebonack Necks upon ye Penalty of Six Shillings a Lode...The Indians Excepted.[14]

Despite the trustees setting aside woodlots at both Shinnecock and Sebonac Necks for the exclusive use by the 200 or so Shinnecock residing there, there were apparently based upon the repeated requests for additional wood leases. Complaints were made by the Indians themselves of tribal members illegally selling timber from tribal leased landsand the Shinnecock's were over-harvesting and mismanaging their timber reserves. All timber except that used by the Indians "for firing and fencing" was reserved to the town in the 1703 1,000 year lease. Yet, the town tried to help the Shinnecock out of their predicament. In 1744, the Southampton town trustees leased to the Indians for fifty years, additional timber rights within the Indian leased lands,

> July 3, 1744 At a trustee meting held at the Schoolhouse voted on sd day that the indians shall have a mile of timber laid to them *from the Conueplace Eastward* Lying on the north sid of ye Path bounded north by the sound South by the path west by the Conuplace dich the East bounds is to be a north Line from the mile tree by the path also Great neck that is Shenecock also Seboneck great Neck: also voted on sd day that the above sd timber that is to be laid to the indians shal be by a Leas to sd Indians for fifty year to com ....that there shall be no Green timber Cut or Carted in any part of the Land that is voted to be laid for the periculer use of the

Indians on foriture of 6s: pr load for any Person so cutting or Carting any Green timber…[15]

This lease only included timber on the 1703 Indian leased lands east of Canoe Place. This was the first of a series of timber leases granted by the town to the Shinnecock in order to supply their needs. Three years later the town trustees further refined the leased timber land boundaries and extended the term of the Indians woodlot lease east of Canoe Place to 100 years. The Shinnecock also asked that three of the trustees lay out individual woodlots for each of the tribal members. The Shinnecock were allowed by the town to select the trustees to lay out these lots for them.[16] Additionally, the town allowed these lots to be held by the Shinnecock for 100 years.

> June, 2, 1747, At a Trustee meeting holden at the Meeting House on the Second day of Jun 1747: it Was then ordered and Enacted by the Trustees of Souuthampton that the Shenecock Indians shall have all the timber in Shenecock Great neck for their own Proper use and also all the timber in Sebonack neck and also one half of the residue of the timber Groing on all the Indian land as followeth that is to say their part of the timber is Ly on the north side from the Conneuplace ditch eastward as far as the Coldspring and althho' It shall extend no farther Eastward then the sd Coldspring yet it shall Contain half the green timber as above sd As it shall be Laid outt or divided of to said Indians by John howell Esq'r Capt Theophilus Howell and Left. Arthur Howell being elected chosen By the Indians to be Layer out of sd timber and the said John Howell Esq'r and Abraham Hallsey appointed by the trustees as above sd and it is to be and remaine to sd Indians & yr sucessers a hundrd years.

The described lease area was in close proximity to the Shinnecock's main village at Cold Spring which was located to the east of Canoe Place at Sebonac.

"the above Indians shall Improve"

Some forty-four years after the enactment of the 1,000 year lease agreement, assimilative change can be discerned by the appearance of individually-held wood lots by members of the Shinnecock community. Even more indicative of cultural change was the inheritance rights bestowed upon the individual recipient. The notion of communally-held lands, long a hallmark of Long Island Indian culture, was yielding to the concept of privately-held inheritable land.

Since August 17, 1703 and the citing of Pomgomo, Chice and Mahanaman as the collective leaders of the Shinnecock, no mention was made in the historical record of an effective tribal leadership. Complaints received by the town trustees were those by individual Shinnecock. Actions taken by the town were taken on the basis of requests by individuals or small groups of Shinnecock individuals. In 1790 the town trustees granted permission to "Samuel Wacus, Samuel Peter, Simeon Fittum, Joseph Killis, Jonathan Tony, Thomas Tony, Abraham Jacob, Jack Mars, Archibald Freeman& Hugh Jonathan" to erect a fence near Cold Creek "for the purpose of plowing &planting" in addition to "the privilege of pasturing Shinecok Neck &Sebonak Neck for three years from this date..." This action was undertaken on the direct request of the named Shinnecock. No Shinnecock political leader was mentioned or present during the proceedings.[17]

Another such indication of the lack of a functioning Shinnecock leadership was the fact that upon the leased lands, it was the town trustees who were laying out "how many acres each family or individual of the above Indians shall Improve and stake off to each one."[18] Normally, following traditional practice, such a role was ascribed to a sachem to perform. There were other indications of a lack of a functioning political authority amongst the Shinnecock community members.

By 1764 both land and timber became an issue among the Shinnecock as did their inability to enforce community-sanctioned standards of behavior. The earlier 1747 allotment of timber rights to individual tribal members had led to the sale of timber located on the 1747 leased lands by individual Shinnecock to local townsmen. The result was a growing shortage of timber resources for the Shinnecock community,

> June 12, 1764, Whereas some particular Indians and Squaws of the tribe belonging to Shinnecock have in times past have hired out land to the English to plant and sow upon to the great damage of the whole. Now it be known to all people to whom it may concern that we whose names are hereunto written Indians and Squaws belonging to Shinnecock do mutually agree that for the future no Indian or squaw shall hire out any land to plant or sow upon in any case whatsoever without the consent of the whole or the major part and if it should be thought proper that any land should be hired out by the Generallity of the Indians there the money arising from such hire shall be equally divided among the whole and if any Indian or squaw shall hire out any land contrary to the intent of this agreement then he or she or they shall forfeit forty shillings for every acre hired out to be discovered by any two or more that will prosecute before any of his majesties Justices and the money when recovered after the charge is paid for prosecution shall be equally divided among those that hve not ----Further neither shall any Indian or squaw sell any timber on penality of eight shillings for any trees so sold the money to be ---as in the case of the land above In Witness whereof we have hereunto set our hands and seals this 12th day of June Anno Dom, 1764
> Simeon Tilum Peter Indian Sam Tilum James Tilum Ralph Indian Solomon Indian Widow Lot Dan Indian Sarah Tutt Samuel Wakus Jenny Gonnock Hannah Wakus Liss Tony Hannah Tim Susy Nero Sue Jacob An Wakus Hannah Peter Seb Charles Phebe Peter Elisabeth Wakus Sarah Norriss Moll

Tony Phebe Hugh Hannah Solomon Kate Musket Mary Warrose Sarah Jo Dinah Harry Nabbi Musket Eunice Chicken Mary Ralph Peter John Phebe Harry Susy Tut Nab Gorin[19]

There were thirty-two signatories to this document, of whom nine were male and twenty-three were female, of an Indian community numbering around 300. No leader, informal or otherwise, was identified in the document. It suggests that there was no adequate tribal authority present to address this community timber sale and land leasing problem, or as noted above, to enforce community standards of behavior, thus the independent actions of the above named group of Shinnecock. In order to accomplish their goal, these petitioners had to request the town's assistance to ensure that community members complied with the agreements made amongst themselves regarding these resources. Yet this measure was not to succeed. In 1782 the same issue was again raised,[20]

> April 30,1782, Indians Complain.- Voted and ordered by said Trustees That Whereas the Indians Complain that they have at Sundry times come int an a greement with each other not to Sell any Wood, or to hire out any Land to the White People which rules of agreement have been broken through and not answered their intention. They have once more entered into a written Agreement by Subscribing their names under penalties and Sanctions not to hire out any of their land or Sel any Wood to the White People on any pretense whatsoever. And have made Application to us the Trustees desiring we would aid and Assist them that there might be a Strict Observance of sd. Agreement.
>
> We therefore the Trustees do Ordor and Enact that there not be any Wood cut on or Carted off any part of the Indian land on penalty of 20/ pr load for Every load so cut on or carted off Except it be for such persons as have Interest in sd. Lands. And then onely for their own Consumption.

What is apparent throughout this period was that Southampton continued to exert its authority over the lands leased to the Shinnecock. The exceptions stated in the 1703 lease only allowed for a restricted or limited degree of Shinnecock occupation and activity. The town retained ownership of all the lands involved. The town trustees on the other hand exerted their authority in accordance with the exceptions provision of the 1703 lease.

At the same time the town continually took actions to protect those lands being utilized by the Shinnecock. The town also assisted the Shinnecock by allowing for the leasing of additional timber lands east of Canoe Place for the Shinnecocks' use. The trustees at the Indians' request divided and allotted timber rights within the timber lease lands for the Shinnecock community in an effort to help the Indians conserve their resources. Yet, as has been noted the Shinnecock community was changing. This change was not confined to land and economic activities, but also something deeper, their ideological beliefs.

New Ideologies

Anthropologically, ideology is a system of interdependent ideas held by a particular social group or society. Within this constellation of ideas are shared beliefs, traditions, principles, and mythologies upon which a community organizes itself and defines and justifies socially acceptable behavior. These ideas are accepted as truth or dogma by the majority of the community. For a social group such as the Shinnecock to transition from their traditional "truths" and its associated norms and values to a newer "truth" was no simple task. Above all, a portion of the social group has to come to the mental realization that the old truths are no longer viable, they have become dysfunctional to such a degree within the social group that it feels their world no longer makes sense, to them, it seems chaotic, anomic. As the late anthropologist Clifford Geertz once noted, "Man can adapt to anything his imagination can cope with, but he can not deal with chaos."[21]

For the Shinnecock residing at Sebonac, this realization was gradual, principally as a result of sustained contact with an increasingly dominant Anglo culture and the assimilation of new "truths" by the Shinnecock associated with them. The realization amongst the Shinnecock was that they no longer controlled their own collective destiny, that such a destiny was increasingly being determined by the town of Southampton and a distant provincial government that now had the political power to impose behavioral norms upon the Shinnecock community. At the same time, as noted earlier, a segment of the Shinnecock population began involving itself in the colonial economic system (trade and barter) and animal husbandry (cattle and swine herding, whaling) and technology (weapons, farming implements, and metalworking). New ideas and practices began to take root amongst the Shinnecock, some good (more stable subsistence), some bad (alcohol). Many Shinnecock began adopting Christian surnames and thus began identifying more with colonial society. Additionally, the lack of a functioning community political authority capable of enforcing community standards and behaviors created a moral vacuum that had to be filled.

Whilst many Shinnecock during the course of their exposure to colonial culture had become acquainted with Christianity and its tenets, their own ideological beliefs remained meaningful. Christianity was of no mean significance to them, it was just another strange practice by a strange people. However, once a prevalent feeling took root amongst the Shinnecock that ideologically, things were falling apart, that their ideology was becoming less meaningful, a door for significant change began to open.

"towards finishing their Meetinghouse"

For the Shinnecock this began with the onset of sustained missionary activities by the Presbyterian missionary Azariah Horton in September of 1741.[22] Among the Shinnecock he found a core group who, previous to his efforts, had been baptized by the Reverend Sylvanns White. This small group had joined the Presbyterian congregation in Southampton.[23] Horton, during one of his visits noted,

> Sebboneck, September 2nd, Preached to forty and upwards...Some of the Chief of the Indians consulted together, and told me just before I left them, that they were resolved to break off their evil Ways, especially Sabbath-breaking, and the sin of Drunkeness...eight or ten of them followed me to the Reverend Mr. White's meeting-house....

During his frequent visits, Horton preached to those Shinnecock who felt disconnected not only at Sebonac, but also at their wintering-over villages at Appacock Creek (Cache-bonneck/Quaog) and at Shinnecock Neck. Even more importantly, Horton began teaching his Shinnecock converts to read.

By 1791, the Christian Shinnecock community at Sebonac had grown to the extent to warrant the presence of their own Indian Meeting House at Sebonnac. The Southampton Proprietary Trustees offered a gift to the Shinnecock to assist in its construction,[24]

> Indian Gift.- Memorandom, That on the said day the Indians by their representatives did agree with the trustees that the Proprietors in Commonage shall have the grazing of Shinecok Neck during the whole year 1792 without molestation Which if they the Indians do punctually fulfill We the Trustees do promise to make them a present of

Twenty Pounds towards finishing their Meetinghouse the present to be made on the 1st day of October in the year 1792. But if any of them or their order shall plow in the said Neck during the above term- then no such present wil be made.

In 1809, the Presbyterian missionary Paul Cuffee[25] reported that Sebonac had a population of 109 (down from a 1750 population of 300) individuals including children. Cuffee's baptized Indian congregation consisted of fifteen adult members.

April 5, 1809
By a communication from the pious Paul Cuffee, of the ninth of June last, it appears that he ministers to four different societies. One of these is settled at Montauk, comprehending ninety-seven persons, inclusive of children...Another is at Cold Spring, comprehending nearly the same number of persons with the former: among them are fifteen church members. The third settlement at which he officiates is at Puspatock consisting only of seven families...At Islip, the last place where Paul labors, the congregation is considerable, composed of Indians and free negroes;...

January 26, 1809
The tribe of Chinecock, or Cold Spring consists, including children, of 109 persons or there about. A very remarkable attention to Divine things has been discovered of late at this place, both by whites and people of colour...

Thus the historical record shows that, circa 1809, the Shinnecock had maintained a continuous residential presence of their main settlement at Sebonac for over 207 years. This entry also confirms that by 1809 Coldspring at Sebonc had become a bi-racial community. At the same time, the Shinnecock were becoming more sedentary mainly due mainly to the leased lands and changing subsistence patterns. As a community, the Shinnecock were transforming via the assimilation of new community practices and ideology.

Part of this transformation was the presence of the Indian Meeting House at Sebonac as the center of community identification. At the same time former members of the community sought employment outside the community. There were those who left to join the whaling industry out of Sag Harbor, and those who participated in Southampton's economy as day workers and farm hands or to work land of their own. This necessitated their leaving Sebonac and settling at Shinnecock Neck, which is close to Southampton Town and west of Canoe Place to participate in lumbering activities. As a growing number were Christian converts, this also necessitated the establishment of additional places of worship.

"But being feeble": The Canoe Place Chapel

The Reverend Paul Cuffee was the driving force in the establishment of the Indian Meeting House at Sebonac in 1791. His name has also been associated with a second Indian congregation west of Canoe Place. Cuffee's remains were interred at this location after he died in 1812, but an Indian congregation did not gather there until 1819. Cuffee himself was of Shinnecock ancestry on his father's side.[26] He was born in Brookhaven in 1757. He was ordained as a Presbyterian minister in 1790, and, as noted earlier, he ministered to congregations at Montauk, Cold Spring (Sebonac), Poospatuck, (Brookhaven), and at Islip. During his ministry, Cuffee, as a Christian minister instituted an annual rite of intensification or revivalization amongst his convert Indian flock. It became known as the "June Sunday" ("June Meetings"). According to Earnest Eells, writing in 1939,[27]

> Paul Cuffee left two memorials that live today. The first is the observance of "June Sunday" in the churches he served. This annual occasion has been for almost 150 years a day of home coming, a sort of tribal meeting in both Shinnecock and

Poosepatuck. At times it was regarded as a sort of "Indian Fair" and hawkers and peddlers took advantage of the crowds to set up stands. Of late it has been, as Cuffee intended it to be, a religious occasion, and its observance has drawn the life of the reservation more truly around the churches....

Cuffee instituted this annual evanjelical rite at both Poospatuck and Sebonac (Coldspring), and possibly for a short period at Montauk. Cuffee may have been influenced by the presence of the annual summer feast that William Smith, the owner and Lord of St. George's Manor in adjacent Brookhaven held for the Manor's tenants, including those Indians residing on Poospatuck Neck where Cuffee had established a church. William Smith's son was also a minister. The June Meeting represented a further acculturation of the Shinnecock community to a new ideological belief system that transcended the boundaries of all the Indian-black communities within his congregation.

There is no evidence that Paul Cuffee ever maintained tribal relations with the Shinnecock. At the time of his death he was a land-holder in Canoe Place.[28] According to the Reverend Lyman Beecher of Easthampton, "After he died in 1812, the Indians nursed their own souls with only occasional visits by local ministers for encouragement.[29] Nathanel Prime (1845) noted,[30] the church west of Canoe Place was not organized until 1819, seven years after Reverend Cuffee's death.

Prime also noted that this church was organized not by or for the Shinnecock, but by the Long Island Presbytery for its members who resided in that area of Southampton, a distance too distant from the congregation gathered in Southampton township proper.

Additionally, the land upon which this church stood was not Indian land. The location of this church (chapel) was at the bottom of Canoe Place Division Lot #5. In 1739, four Proprietors were allotted commonage rights in this lot, Abram Howell, Abram Howell Jr., Joseph Burnet, and Jonathan Cook.[31] According to the Southampton Town Records[32] the entirety of Lot #5, including this chapel land was purchased on May 16, 1803 by a Moses Culver. He purchased it from Matthew and Phebe Howell. The previous owners of this lot, Elias W. Howell and Nathan Sanford had sold the south end of Canoe Place Division Lot #5 to Samuel Sanford, "for the purpose of erecting a meeting house or church thereon, and also for a burying ground…"[33]

Culver was a deacon in the Presbyterian Church. Culver's attachment to the Presbyterian Church and especially its missionary activities was such that he bequeathed sizable sums of his estate to both the Foreign Presbyterian Missionary Society and the Home Presbyterian Mission Society.[34] It was Culver who allowed the missionary Reverend Cuffee's remains to be buried on his property in 1812 and a chapel later to be erected there.

Prime,[35] as noted earlier, stated that this chapel organized in 1819 "But being feeble and having no stated preaching of house of worship, it has become extinct." When did this extinction occur?

By internal evidence presented in Downs[36] (1887), the Canoe Place Chapel was defunct by 1829. For ten years the Reverend William Benjamin ministered to its congregation. Downs wrote,

> On the 12th of October, 1827, the convention ordained the Rev. William Benjamin as pastor of the Church at Canoe Place, which included Poospatuck and Shinecock…and in the year of 1829 and 1830 I commenced to teach a district school and the Sabbath attended the meeting, where Rev. William Benjamin preached. It was in the Good Ground School House. The Church at Canoe Place was so much decayed the

Old Presbyterian Church and the Indian Church held their meetings together....

While the above is of historical interest, what is important to note is that there were two congregations utilizing this chapel. The Indian congregation consisted of both Shinnecock and Poospatuck Indians. Prime, in his appendices (Appendix 1) noted the total Indian membership came to 70, "Canoe Place ...membs. 70." The land upon which they congregated was owned by Southampton resident Moses Culver, who allowed the Indians to use it.

When the church was abandoned, the joint Indian congregations moved to the schoolhouse at "Goodground" (present-day Westhampton) where they combined with the non-Indian congregation. So united, they prayed together as one. One further point to note was that this chapel represented a permanent dispersal of Shinnecock from Sebonac into the larger community. Were there others?

"the tribe had a church": The "Warnertown" Chapel

The following listing states "Warnertown (Canoe Place)...membs. 12." Warnertown was south of the present-day Montauk Highway on the west shore of Shinnecock Bay. Two locations were being serviced by the Reverend William Benjamin who had previously ministered to the Poosapatuck/Shinnecock congregation at Good Ground. It is clear that this Appendix was referring to a new Shinnecock congregation that had gathered on Shinnecock Neck, which in 1859, was to become the Shinnecock community's home. Prime[37] spoke of Shinnecock Neck, (c.1845), as the "the residence of the remnants of the Shinnecock tribe of Indians." According to Downs,[38] the Reverend Benjamin Downs paid $250.00 out of his own funds to construct the chapel on the Neck.

As noted above, the second Shinnecock chapel was also in the Canoe Place region. This chapel, cited by Prime,[39] was located on Shinnecock Bay, south of the present-day Montauk Highway on Canoe Place Road. This congregation was an offshoot of the congregation that met at the schoolhouse at Good Ground. Circa 1845 Prime[40] noted:

> A small Congregational church, under the name of Warnertown, still exists in this vicinity, which consists of only 12 members.

The Reverend James Y. Downs was servicing this chapel in 1877 when, due to a dwindling congregation, Downs "discontinued" his activities there. Of interest, Reverend William Benjamin who previously ministered to the Poospatuck/Shinnecock congregation at Good Ground also, as he did at Shinnecock Neck, contributed $250.00 of his own money to construct the Warnertown chapel for the Indians' use.[41]

According to Prime,[42] in 1845 this congregation consisted of twelve members. Charles Bunn[43] a Shinnecock (age 86, 1953, b.1867) testified on the basis of oral tradition that "...the tribe had a church on the strip which was used for public religious services before 1859...." If Bunn's data is correct, Indians were using the chapel built with the funds provided by the Reverend William Benjamin after he had left the mixed Good Ground congregation. We know from the Prime Appendix that this was circa 1845.

The Church at Shinnecock Neck

It was mentioned earlier that the Shinnecock were, by 1747, utilizing portions of present-day Shinnecock Neck for timber, herding, and agriculture. The Neck, in addition to the traditional wintering-over village at Quag, also became a convenient wintering-over site. As time progressed, a year-round Indian population appeared at Shinnecock Neck in addition to those at Sebonac. For example, in 1796[44] the town trustees marked out 190 acres of land for the Shinnecock's use at Sebonac Neck but no land was so-demarcated at Shinnecock Neck. In 1813, the Shinnecock at Sebonac had ninety acres of land under cultivation.[45] But during 1816, the Shinnecock had 100 acres laid out by the town trustees for their use upon Shinnecock Neck.[46] Clearly the Sebbonac Shinnecock population was decreasing, dispersing west of Canoe Place and south to Shinnecock Neck.

By 1824, the Reverend William Benjamin, who was ministering to Indian congregations at Canoe Place and Westhampton, established a church for the Indians at Shinnecock Neck. Like the Warnertown chapel, the Reverend Benjamin used his own funds to establish and construct the first church at Shinnecock Neck.[47] He remained their pastor until his death in 1860. What did all of these meeting houses, chapels, and churches have in common besides their ethnic make-up? They were all built with funds donated by the Shinnecock's neighbors, the town and residents of Southampton. These meeting houses and chapels were also a testament to the growing acceptance of Christianity amongst the Shinnecock and their growing acculturation to colonial norms and values.

"we will give them al Shinnecock Neck"

Adding significance to the establishment of the church at Shinnecock Neck were the minutes of a town trustee meeting held in Southampton on April 11, 1826,[48]

> Voted that if the Indians agree, we will give them al Shinnecock Neck as it is now fenced & they to fence the Neck to secure themselves.

There is no evidence in the town Indian records that the Shinnecock accepted this proposal. The town's Indian records do not contain any further information concerning this gift proposal. Neither do the Southampton town records.[49] At this point in time the town of Southampton was willing to give the Shinnecock most of Shinnecock Neck in return for their lease lands within the Shinnecock Hills area. Yet we find that at the next trustee meeting (April 25), the Trustees had a fence erected at the top of Shinnecock Neck ("the ditch") and allowed twelve cattle to graze there. At the May 17 trustee meeting, a Shinnecock was allowed to graze his horse on the Neck, provided that, "he to be faithful in Keeping the Neck clear of trespass and to inform of anyone in leaving the Gate open."[50] This was yet another example of the town and the Shinnecock's willingness to cooperate in sharing resources, be it natural or human.

At the same time, the Shinnecock allowed an important opportunity to have their own land base at Shinnecock Neck slip between their collective fingers. Luckily for the Shinnecock, some thirty-six years later, this opportunity was to again be offered.

VIII. A New Form of Government

"we would aid and Assist them"

Previously, it was noted that there was no clear indication of a functioning political leadership amongst the Shinnecock at Sebonac after the 1703 lease agreement. On the basis of a series of documents presented, it was clear that the Shinnecock Sebonac community could not maintain internal control of itself due to this lack of an effective political authority. This situation still persisted in 1782 when the town trustees noted,[1]

> Indians Complain.- Voted and ordered by the said Trustees That Whereas the Indians Complain that they have a t Sundry times come int an a greement with each other not to Sell any Wood, or to hire out any Land to the White People which rules of agreement have been broken thrugh and not answered their intention. They have once more entered into a written Agreament by Subscribing their names under penalties and Sanctions not to hire out any of their land or Sel any Wood to the White People on any pretense whatsoever. And have made Application to us the Trustees desiring we would aid and Assist them that there might be a Strict Observance of sd. Agreement.
> We therefore the Trustees do Ordor and Enact that there not be any Wood cut on or Carted off any part of the Indian land on penalty of 20/ pr load for Every load so cut on or carted off Except it be for such persons as have Interest in sd. Lands. And then onely for their own Consumption.

As in previous situations the town was called upon by groups of individual Shinnecock asking the town's assistance to ensure order within the Indian community. Again the Shinnecock were unable to assert internal control over the residents of their community.

On April 6, 1790, nine individual Shinnecock requested permission from the town trustees to erect a fence and gates in the Cold Creek area of Shinnecock Hills near Sebonac, "for the purpose of plowing and planting."[2] In granting this request the town trustees,

> Also voted that the above Indians in addition to the above mentioned agreement be allowed to fence as above on the condition that they chuse two men white or black to associate with a third man chosen by the Trustees for the time being who shall go and lay out said field yearly and order how many acres each family or individual of the above Indians shall Improve or stake off to each one and if said Indians have a mind to let others of the natives of Shinecok plow in their enclosed field the said three men shall lay out for them in like manner as above.

First, the trustees were clearly discriminating between Indians and mixed Indian-Blacks or "mullatoes" within the Shinnecock community. Second, the trustees clearly desired that the Shinnecock community begin regulating their own use of the leased lands allotted to them rather than have individuals independently come to the town trustees with each and every request. That the Shinnecock complied with the trustees request is indicated in the following 1791 entry in the trustee records,[3]

> Indian Gift.- Memorandom, That on the said day the Indians by their representatives did agree with the trustees that the Proprietors in Commonage shall have the grazing of Shinecok Neck during the whole year 1792 without molestation Which if they the Indians do punctually fulfill We the Trustees do promise to make them a present of Twenty Pounds towards finishing their Meetinghouse the present to be made on the 1st day of October in the year 1792. But if any of them or their order shall plow in the said Neck during the above term- then no such present wil be made.

A New Form of Government

For the first time since 1703 there was a direct meeting between individuals recognized as representing the needs of the Shinnecock community and those representing the town of Southampton. The Shinnecock, with the political support of the town, took this representative structure one step further by petitioning the New York State Legislature in 1792 to legislate a limited form of leadership via statutory enactment,[4]

> Mr L'Hommedieu, from the Committee to whom was referred the petition of Samuel Wakas, and other Indians of the Shinnecock Tribe residing in Suffolk county and praying the interposition of the legislature, for the regulation of the tillage of their common lands, reported, that it was the opinion of the Committee, that it will be proper to afford relief to the petitioners, and that a bill be ordered to be bought in for that purpose, which report he read in his place and delivered the same in at the table, there it was again read and agreed to by the Senate. Thereupon
>
> Ordered, That the same committee do prepare and bring in a bill accordingly....

On February 24, 1792, the requested legislation was enacted into law by the New York General Assembly,[5]

> Be it enacted by the People of the State of New York, represented in Senate and Assembly, and it is hereby enacted by the authority of the same. That it shall and may be lawful for the male Indians of twenty-one years of age and upwards, belonging to the Shinnecock tribe in Suffolk county, to meet together on the first Tuesday in April next, and on the first Tuesday in April in every year thereafter, at the place for holding town meetings in the town of Southampton, and there by a plurality of voices, to choose three persons belonging to the said tribe as trustees, who by and with the consent of three justices of the peace residing next to the lands of the said Shinnecock tribe, are hereby authorized and empowered from time to time to lease out so much of the said lands as they shall judge proper for the use of the said tribe, for any term not exceeding three years, and to lay out and appropriate such

quantity of said land to each family or individual, as shall be judged necessary for his or their improvements.

And it be further enacted by the authority aforesaid, That it shall be the duty of the clerk of the town of Southampton, annually to attend and preside at the meeting of the said Indians for choosing said trustees, and to enter in a book to be by him kept for that purpose the names of the persons who shall be so chosen trustees as aforesaid.

And it be further enacted by the authority aforesaid, That if any person or persons whosoever, shall plough or otherwise improve any of the lands belonging to the said tribe, without the consent of a majority of the said trustees and a majority of the said Justices first had and obtained in writing and entered in the book herein directed to be kept by the said Clerk such person or persons shall severally forfeit the sum of forty shillings for every acre so occupied, notwithstanding he or they may have obtained licence to improve the said land or any part thereof from any Indian or Indians of the said tribe to be recovered with costs of suit in their own names in any court having cognizance of the same.

This law recognized a limited political authority of the Shinnecock regarding eligibility, land management, and allotment of land within the leased area via the annual election of three Indian trustees by qualified Shinnecock community voters. A record of these proceedings was to be maintained by the Southampton town clerk. These trustee's actions were still subject to town authority via the approval or rejection of their actions by a committee consisting of three town justices of the peace.

One of the first of the trustee-directed actions setting aside land to be allotted was taken at an Indian trustee meeting held on April 6, 1793,[6]

> Motion seconded if the Indian Tribe Shall have their planting field apportioned out in Sebbonak great neck Voted in the affirmative So voted that there be allowed a garden to every

house or wigwam that is inhabited for the summer not exceeding half an acre.... Voted that Caleb Cooper & William Herrick shall go into Sebonak great neck & measure off an take off and mark & number 150 or 190 acres & make report to the trustees at their next meeting....

Additionally, a proceeding was recorded by the town at a Shinnecock trustee meeting held on April 9, 1793, wherein the trustees enacted regulations concerning land allotments within the Sebonnac Neck lease area,[7]

> The Indians met agreeable to the law provided in that case and voted in three Trustees viz Abraham Jacob, David Jacob & Absalom Cuffee pr Wm Herrick Clerk. (April 2 1793)
>
> At a meeting held by the Trustees of __ Indian tribe of Shinnecocks & the trustees after mentioned in Southampton on the 9th Day of April Anno 1793 was voted as follows:
>
> 1st That no one family or individual shall plow more than six acres.
>
> 2d That if any Indian or Indians shall fail to do their proportion of the Fence they shall be curtailed of the land allotted to them at the discretion of the Committee hereafter appointed.
>
> 3rd That no person or persons on the pretense of having hired land of Indians who are gone to sea or otherwise absent shall challenge or improve any lands which may be laid out to their wives or families on penalty of forfeiture which the law directs.
>
> 4ly That Abraham Jacob, David Jacob and Absalom Cuffee stand a Committee to lay out land to be plowed this Spring for planting at their discretion not exceeding the limits abovementioned.
>
> > Caleb Cooper
> > Obadiah Rogers
> > Uriah Rogers Trustees
> > Absalom Cuffee
> > Abraham Jacob

David Jacob

Continued cooperation between the town and Shinnecock trustees was evident wherein meetings between the trustees of both the Shinnecock and Southampton were held as necessary, as noted in a March 5, 1793 entry in the town trustee records,[8]

> Indians.- Also voted that Caleb Cooper Esqr. Go to the Indians at Cold Spring & invite them to attend at the next trustee Meeting.

The following October such a meeting was also necessitated,[9]

> Shinecoc Neck.- Voted and ordered that Capt. Abraham Saye & Caleb Cooper Esquire be appointed to confer with the Indians about the day to turn Creatures into Shinecock & notify the Proprietors and that Hugh Gelston & Samuel Cooper be Inspectors of said neck for the remaining part of the season-....

At times the Shinnecock rented portions of their lease lands to town residents, [10]

> We the Subscribers Natives of Shinnecocks for and in consideration of Twenty Shillings per Acre to us paid in Hand, do hire out to Uriah Rogers, as many acres of land as is affixed to our hands & seals, for to said lands for next year and the year after next and no longer- And we promise to warrant & Defend Said Lands from any other Person or Persons as we are the true and lawful heirs to said land, we dispose of the same for the use abovementioned
>
> As witness our hands & seals in Southampton
>
> This Twelfth Day of November 1793

Or, they divided land allotments amongst themselves or for the Shinnecock in general for the coming season,

> 1 Acre Mary Joe,1Acre Lunae Pattaguam,1 ½ Acre George Hanibal, 1 Acre Peg Ruckets, 3 Acres Sarah Acres, 3 Acres Joseph Kellis, Two Acres Sarah Titus, Two Acres Bethiah

Jethro, One Acre Abigail Solomon, Two Acres Prudence Cuffee, 1 Acre Phebe Ralph, Two Acres Elizabeth Manaman, 1 Acre William Briston, 1 Acre Edward Molly Murrain.

At an Indian Trustees Meeting held at the house of Zebulon Howel in Southampton by a majority of the Justices & a majority of the Trustees who were present was voted as follows.

First that Caleb Cooper Esq. together with the three Indian trustee be a Committee from this house to Lay out Shinnecock Neck and Little Neck if it shall be deemed to be necessary for the use of the tribe this season-into acres.

2ndly Voted that said Committee begin to lay out on Thursday the 10th of this instant or if stormy the Next fair day.

3rdly Voted that there be allowed a garden to every house and wigwam that is inhabited for the summer not exceeding half an acre, and if any person shall plow or improve more than half an Acre for a house or wigwam, they shall forfeit as the Act directs & be prosecuted by these justices…[11]

Thus, those Shinnecock community members who having having met the requirements set down by the Indian trustees would then have acreage set aside for their use. The land itself was subject to the regulation by the trustees as noted by this November 1793 action,[12]

Allotment of Indian lands.
1 Acre Harry Joe	3 acres Sarah Ocus
1 acre Susie Pattaquam	2 acres Joseph Killis
1 ½ acre Peg Jordan	2 acres Sarah Silas
1 acre George Hannabal	2 acres Bethiah Jethro
1 acre Peg Ruchets	2 acres Prudence Cuffee
1 acre Phebe Ralph	1 acre Abigail Solomon
2 acres Prudence Cuffee.	2 acres Elisabeth Manaman
1 acre William Boyton	1 acre Edwerd Murrian

(24 1/2 acres total)

Scarcity of tillable land was not a problem for the Shinnecock within the 1703 leased lands. As needs increased, land was readily available to utilize,[13]

Indian Trustee Meeting, April 14, 1794.
...Also voted that the Indians have a Blank Lot laid out west from Great Hill South to the Road, & to extend as far West as Rocky Point-, for the benefit of the tribe also voted that Shinnecock & Little Neck be laid out into acres, that if Shinnecock Should fall short of the quantity of land necessary it may be made up in Little neck and if both fall short then the deficiency to be made up in the Blank lot.

Indian Trustee Meeting, April 28, 1794.
At a meeting of the Trustees of the Indian tribe with the Trustees--. Proceeded as follows-----\
Whereas there are a number of Acres yet left in little Neck & Shinnecock undrawn. Be it enacted that Abraham Cuffee who was left out in the other draft He shall take one acre of ground in Shinnecock & the other in Little Neck & run his chance for the tird, & Prudence Cuffee is to have an acre in Shinnecock & another in little Neck, And those whose names are underwritten, are to put all their names into one hat and the trustees are to lay out as many Acres as they can find in both Necks and number the acres...Simeon [H]iturn, Abraham Cuffee, Solomon Porheg, William C[], Gilbert Williams, Joshuah Hugh, Mary Tu [ff]s, Harry Jacob, Nab Solomon, Peg Ruckets, Harry Joel, Hannah Thene, Elizabeth Durees, Eunice Pattaquams.

Indian Trustee Meeting, April 19, 1798
...That the Indians have 80 acres more in some field...

Indian Trustee Meeting, April 22, 1807
Voted that Indians plow 90 acres this year to be apportioned out to individuals as hereafter directed.

The minutes of the preceding meeting verify the availability of planting ground for the Shinnecock and the ability for it to expand as the need arose. Land availability for agricultural use was not an issue within the 1703 leased lands.

Several problems facing the Shinnecock trustees was of non-Indian town residents marrying an Indian and claiming land allotment rights, and non-resident Shinnecock laying similar claims before the Indian trustees. In 1799 the Shinnecock trustees addressed both problems,[14]

> At a meeting held at the house of Paul Sayre by the Indian trustees was voted as follows That, No person not being an original proprietor shall draw any land by virtue of marrying a Squaw. But the squaw shall draw the same as any other Squaw who is a proprietor.
> 2nd – Voted that a squaw who is not a native if she shall marry an Indian shall draw equally with any other squaw who is a native & have equal privileges-
> 3rd – voted that no Indian or squaw who belong to the tribe If they do not reside within the township shall be considered In the draft of land which is this Spring to made for planting.
> 4th- Notwithstanding the above It is voted that every Indian or squaw who belong to the tribe if they are non-residents shall be entitled to half as much land as those who reside in the town according to their right which shall be allotted to them by the trustees…

The 1792 legislation enacted to establish the Shinnecock trustee system was amended on April 4, 1801 by the New York State Legislature so as to further protect the Shinnecock and their resources. In part this legislation read,[15]

> …said tribe are hereby authorized and impowered from time to time to lease out so much of the said lands, as they shall judge proper for the benefit of the said tribe, for any term not exceeding three years, and to lay out and appropriate such quantity of the said lands to each individual or family of the said tribe as they shall judge proper for his or their improvement, and also to order and direct on what part of the said lands firewood and timber may be cut by the said tribe for their own use…

> ...and if any person shall occupy or use any of the said lands without the consent of the majority of the said trustees and the majority of such justices first obtained and entered in the said book, such person shall forfeit the sum of five dollars for every acre so used or occupied, and any person belonging to the said tribe, shall cut any wood or timber on the said lands without such order and consent of the said trustees and justices first entered in the said book, such person shall forfeit the sum of ten dollars for each offence shall be sued for and recovered by such justices in their own names in any court having cognizance thereof with costs of the suit, for the use of the said tribe.

Besides the state legislature, in 1818, the town trustees also, on the behalf of their Shinnecock counterparts took further action to protect the Shinnecock's leased lands and resources not only from non-Indians, but also from some of the Shinnecock,[16]

> ...Also from Indian land.- and be it further enacted, that from and after the passing of this Act, it shall not be lawful for any person or persons (other than the Indian tribe) to Cut or take any wood, or brush from any part of the Indian Lands, on any pretense whatever without the consent of the sd. Trustees...
> ...Indian Not to Cut but for their own use.- and be it further enacted, that from and after the passing of this Act, it shall not be lawful for any person or persons belonging to the Indian tribe, to cut any wood or brush on any of the Indian Lands (the fee of which is invested to the Proprietors) except for his or her own use for building, firing, fencing, broom and basket stuff &c., and any person or persons of the said Indian tribe, who shall be found cutting wood or brush on the said Land other than for the purpose aforesaid, shall be deemed guilty of a trespass, and shall be liable to a prosecution before any legal and proper Court having cognizance thereof.

By 1813, the trustees were also differentiating between rights of those communities residing still at Sebbonac and the community at Shinnecock Neck. At their April 12, 1813 meeting[17] the trustees voted specific rights for those Shinnecock residing on Shinnecock Neck,

> Voted that no person or persons shall cut any brush in Shinnecock Excepth those who reside in the Neck Without the consent of the trustees under penalty of the law.

Having had the institution of Shinnecock trustee sanctioned by a state law, the Shinnecock trustees now had the force of New York state law to back up their regulations.

The emergence of a new, recognized Shinnecock leadership was the result of a cooperative effort by both the town of Southampton and the Shinnecock community. The appearance of the Shinnecock trustees greatly facilitated peaceful relations between the two communities. At this point in time, the role played by these trustees was restricted by state legislation to land allotment-related issues. During this same time period there is no record of a specific functioning community leadership that asserted its authority over the entirety of the Shinnecock community.

Racial and Ethnic Tensions

As noted earlier, one of several problems facing the Shinnecock community was of non-Indian town residents marrying an Indian and claiming land allotment rights and non-resident Shinnecock laying similar claims before the town trustees the Shinnecock trustees. Other related issues also arose that had to be addressed by both the community and the town. First amongst them was the issue of race.

By 1800, the practice of freeing slaves had accelerated in southern New England and on Long Island. As a result many of these recently released slaves sought residence within and married into Indian communities. The result was the emergence of bi-racial and sometimes tri-racial communities such as those at Golden Hill, Mashantucket, Niantic,

Narragansett, Lantern Hill, and Mashpee in southern New England. On Long Island the same process appeared at Montauk, Poospatuck, and at Shinnecock. Affected Indian communities responded in three different ways, by allowing residence and integration into the community, exclusion and in-marriage prohibitions such as was practiced on the Mohegan reservation in Connecticut, or by removal to new Indian communities such as the Brotherton community, which was a polyglot Indian community that erected ethnic barriers that excluded both blacks and mulattoes, a practice that continues to this day.

Second, was the out-migration of mulattoes (Indian-Black) from Indian enclaves only to settle at other Indian communities.

The Shinnecock, with the town's assistance appeared to apply a limited exclusion rule, that is, allowing in-marriage, but excluding blacks and mulattoes who had no familiar relations to the Shinnecock community. The town trustees addressed this issue by preventing such individuals, having no direct community ties, from receiving Shinnecock land allotments. On April 1, 1806, the town trustee records first took note of this issue:[18]

> Voted, That Ebenezer Howel be appointed to notify *Absalon Cuffee, Bun, and the several branches of that family,* to meet with the Trustees on Tuesday next at H. Rogers and give them satisfaction respecting their title to the Indian Land, or otherwise they shall be debarred drawing any land this season...

Both the town and Shinnecock trustees were cognizant of the fact that Bun was a fee slave who married a Poospatuck Indian and Absalom Cuffee, a mulatto, who, like Bun, was originally a resident of the Indian community at Poospatuck in Brookhaven and had come to Southampton. In both instances neither family could claim any allotment right to Shinnecock leased lands within Southampton.

"Debarred from drawing"

One week later, these two families, Cuffee family members, and other named individuals were denied any allotment rights to the Shinnecock lands,[19]

> Debarred from drawing.-22d. Voted, That Absalon Cuffee, Abraham Cuffee, Noah Cuffee, James Bun, Simeon Fithen, Ton Jock, Jason Cuffee, Meshec Cuffee along with their respective families be debarred drawing any land among the Indians this season, unless they first satisfy the Trustees with respect to their title in the said lands. Indians.- 4thly. Voted that Caleb Cooper Esqr., Capt David Rose, and William Herrick be a Committee to consult such persons as they suppose will be able to give them any information respecting the business now pending with the Indians, and make report to the Trustees.

The following October both the town and Shinnecock trustees came to an understanding based on a legal opinion proffered by the town justices,[20]

> Having perused the preceding lease I am of the opinion in answer to questions proposed to me

> That no person can claim any right or interest by virtue of the lease excepting Indians so called, and that neither negroes mulattoes nor whites are comprehended within the general description of the persons to whom the lease was made.

In order to enforce this united understanding against attempts by non-community members to sue to obtain an Indian allotment and to protect the Shinnecock and their trustees from any such suit, the town and Shinnecock trustees passed, with the concurrence of the town proprietors, the following in 1815,[21]

Voted. That if the Justices & Indian Trustees shall deny any persons Indian Land for planting not allowing such suspected persons liberty to draw. And in consequence of denial, they should be prosecuted, by the sd. Applicants, or their representatives then, the Trustees of the Town, do hereby engage at the expense of the Proprietors, to indemnify the said Indian trustees, and defend the suit. And have authorized Genl. Abraham Rose, & William Herrick Esqr. As our advocates, at their discretion and at the expense of the proprietors, to avail themselves of every legal measure to bring the business to a final issue.

On April 14, 1815, the Shinnecock trustees, the town trustees, as well as the town magistrates stood together to confront this continued issue,[22]

At a meeting of the Magistrates of the Town of Southampton & the Indian Trustees held April 19th 1815...
Voted that Hannah Cuff, Paul Cuff, Vincent Cuff, Polly Dyer, Polly Dick, Sukey Dyer shall be debarred from having any land voted that this meeting be adjourned to the evening of Drawing the land.
James Posr Clerk, Wm Herrick, David Rose, James Pierson Justices.
David Walkus, Jonatathon Tony Trustees.

The preceding continued to depict the ability and willingness of the town and the Shinnecock community to work together to address common problems. The data presented conflicts with the often-stated view that the town of Southampton was obsessed in riding itself of its Indian population and obtaining all of their lands. In reality, the Shinnecock community became a necessary part of the town's economy by providing labor for farming and commercial timber harvesting as well as assisting in natural resource management. By the actions of both the Shinnecock and town trustees, they, together, protected the lands that they shared from unwarranted intrusion, use, and occupation.

Land Problems

Why was there such sensitivity by both the town and the Shinnecock community to outsiders settling within the community? It would seem odd that Southampton and the Shinnecock would exclude individuals from land allotments, especially amongst the named Cuffee family, who, in large part were descendents of the Reverend Paul Cuffee. Cuffee, it will be remembered, was related to the Shinnecock via his paternal line, although he never resided within this Indian community. The issue boiled down to land availability.

Southampton was a growing town with a growing non-Indian population. Pressure for expanded settlement within the Shinnecock Hills region of the town was also growing. Land for settlement had to be provided, but also the town had to protect the rights of the Shinnecock gained from the 1703 Shinnecock Hills lease.

At this point in time, the Shinnecock had the 1747 100 year lease right to a one mile square of timber land within the Shinnecock Hills/Sebonac area for their timber needs.[23] Additionally, the trustees gave the Shinnecock full timber rights to all of Sebonac and Shinnecock Necks. This land was in addition to those lands annually allotted for agriculture and grazing varied in size from year to year. For instance, at the April 13, 1813 trustee meeting 90 acres were allotted for agricultural use. At the April 4, 1815 trustee meeting 100 acres were so-allotted. The minutes of the April 4, 1816 meeting also had 108 acres set aside to be allotted.[24] These agricultural allotment lands were in addition to the lands encompassing the Shinnecock community village sites at Sebbonac (Cold Spring) and on Shinnecock Neck. As noted in the April 25, 1815 trustee meeting minutes, any remaining un-allotted lands could be "hired out" (leased) to non-Indians.

In order to ensure adequate agricultural lands for the Shinnecock population, the New York State Assembly enacted a revised version of the April 4, 1801 Shinnecock legislation in 1810. In this revision, the Shinnecock were guaranteed to have up to 125 acres of land allotted to them for agricultural use. In 1816, this law was again amended.[25] The acreage stipulation remained, but stiffer penalties were provided in Section III of the Act for non-Indians (25 dollars for each acre) who encroached upon and used Shinnecock allotted lands without the permission of the trustees.

> And it be further enacted, That if any person not of the said tribe shall in any manner hire, use or occupy any of the said lands, which shall be so laid out and appropriated as aforesaid, such person shall forfeit the sum of twenty-five dollars for every acre so hired, used, or occupied; and if any person shall occupy or use any of the said lands, without the consent of the majority of the said trustees, and of at least two of the said justices first obtained and entered in the said book, such persons shall forfeit the sum of twenty-five dollars for every acre so used or occupied.

In addition to the above, this new enactment provided increased sanctions against members of the Shinnecock community who illegally harvested and sold timber from Shinnecock lands to non-Indians.

> And if any person belonging to the said tribe, shall cut any wood or timber on the said lands without such order and consent of the said trustees and justices first entered into said book, such persons shall forfeit the sum of ten dollars for each offence; the one half of which penalties shall be to the use of the overseers of the poor of the town of Southampton, and the other half to the use of the party who will sue for the same, by the action of debt, in any court having cognizance thereof.

The town was serious about protecting the Shinnecock's timber and agricultural assets. It was noted earlier, that in 1815, Hannah, Paul, and Vincent "Cuff" (Cuffee) along with Polly and Lukey Dyer and Polly Dick were "debarred from having any land" on the basis of their non-membership in the Shinnecock community. In addition, the town prosecuted a number of town residents for encroachment upon Indian lands and for purchasing illegally harvested Indian timber.[26]

"the white people will not allow any of us to vote": The 1822 Petition

According to both the Indian trustee and the town trustee records there appears to have been a lapse of some seven years (1816-1823) of Shinnecock leadership. There were no recorded April Indian trustee elections recorded by the town clerk during this same period. During this time period the town trustees continued to enforce town ordinances against unlawful use and woodcutting on the Indian lease lands and they continued to warn the Shinnecock that their harvesting of timber was, as stipulated in the 1703 conditional leasehold agreement, limited to their own needs, "Indian Not to Cut but for their Own Use" and to reaffirm that the town proprietors were still the owners in fee of the lease lands, "the fee of which is invested in the Proprietors."[27]

Despite this reaffirmation, on January 26, 1822, twelve Shinnecock petitioned the New York State legislature[28] (six of whom were Cuffee's and two were Bun's) claiming that "the Tribe of Indians of Shinecock...are the rightful & lawful owners of a certain tract of land lying in the said Town of Southampton...these lands we claim to be improved by us from the first day of April to the last day of October Annually." Here the petitioners contradict themselves by claiming to be the lawful owners in fee of the tract and then go on to note that their usage rights of the land they claim ownership to was limited to the period of April through October annually.

The petition goes on to explain the seven-year lapse in the Shinnecock trustee system,

> the white people will not allow any of us to vote for such trustees but such persons as May belong to the tribe which deletes almost the whole of us from the privilege we believe belong to us we therefore pray that the law may be so amended as to enable us all to enjoy the privileges…your petitioners further state that we have appointed Noah Cuffee one of our tribe as our agent.

It will be recalled that a legal opinion was previously proffered in 1806 by the town justices, [29]

> Having perused the preceding lease I am of the opinion in answer to questions proposed to me.
>
> That no person can claim any right or interest by virtue of the lease excepting Indians so called, and that neither negroes mulattoes nor whites are comprehended within the general description of the persons to whom the lease was made.

As a result, five named Cuffee's along with their families were "debarred" from any land allotment rights on the basis that they were not considered to be part of the Shinnecock community. Noah Cuffee was amongst them. Another petition signatory, James Bun was similarly debarred.[30] Interestingly, the town Indian records noted that Bun was a Shinnecock trustee beginning in 1801 through 1807 before his rights were challenged, most probably on the basis of his Black/Unkechauge lineage. Likewise, Noah Cuffee was a trustee in 1812 and 1813. Of importance to note was that this petition represented a continuance of the ethnic and racial tensions that began in the early 1800's. What is especially significant was the statement made in the petition that "which deletes almost

A New Form of Government 103

the whole of us from the privilege we believe belong to us." It is a very telling testament to the racial transition that had occurred amongst the Shinnecock prior to 1822. It was so substantial that the petitioners, on the behalf of the Shinnecock asked that the qualifying criteria in the law be changed so that the current membership could qualify to become a trustee.

The town, which recognized only full Shinnecock Indians, not mixed race individuals, responded to the Indian petition by dispatching General Abraham Rose,[31] a town justice of the peace, to address the state legislature presenting the town's position in regard to this issue. The result was that the state legislature did not respond to the Shinnecock petition, but the town on its own volition, did. At the April 1, 1823 Indian-Town meeting, three Indian trustees were elected. Two of the three so-elected were Noah Cuffee and James Bun. Neither the town trustees nor the town justices objected to their election. An amicable resolution of the issue had been achieved.

The question of who was, and conversely, who was not, a Shinnecock continued long after this 1823 resolution, in particular with the Cuffee and Bun lineages. Continued insight into this problem is gained from a review of the military eligibility and enrollment records kept by the town of Southampton, circa 1861-1865. There, five Bunn males of military age (25-34) are listed as residing on the later established (1859) united Shinnecock community at Shinnecock Neck: Russell, David, Franklin, Nelson, and Warren. Out of these five individuals only one (David) qualified for an Indian exemption. The others were listed as "colored" and thus eligible for military service. There were five Cuffee males residing on the reservation of military age (30-40) also cited: James, James L., Luther, Andrew, and Wickham. As with the Bunn males, only one these individuals qualified for an Indian exemption, (Wickham). The other four were similarly declared "colored" and thus eligible for service. A third male group (Lev) consisting of four individuals (ages 27-35) also resided on the reservation. Out of the four only one (Milton Lev) qualified for the Indian exemption. The others were identified as "colored." Indian ancestry was of a significant minority in all three male groups. Two of these family groups, as we have seen (Bun and Cuffee), were both prominent and controversial within the Shinnecock community from the early nineteenth century onwards.

A Changing Community

As noted earlier, the contentious issue between the town and the Shinnecock was based upon a racial transition that had occurred within the Shinnecock community. The question was, based upon a legal interpretation of the 1792 legislative act and the 1703 conditional leasehold agreement, that one of who was and who was not a Shinnecock Indian and a lawful member of that defined community.

What other changes had occurred within and amongst the Shinnecock that also tended to blur and confuse the distinction?

The aboriginal language spoken by the historic Shinnecock Indians at the time of first sustained contact, the key element in the transmittal of tradition and knowledge between succeeding generations, had, by the mid 19th century been forgotten, replaced in turn by the language of the dominant society. French, (1861),[32] noted this total transition to English and abandonment of Indian dialect by the middle of the 19th century.

French[33] also noted the transition from contact era Indian cultural norms, traditions, religion, and forms of governance to those more in line with the then contemporary local society,

Shinnecock, on the E. side of Shinnecock Bay, is an Indian settlement of about 20 homes... This is the residence of the remnant of the Shinnecock Indians, consisting of about 200 persons. They have learned many of the arts of civilized life, and obtain a subsistence by cultivating the soil, fishing, and taking clams. Many of the young men go on whaling voyages, and the young women are employed as servants in the families of the whites. They have entirely lost their native language, and speak English fluently. They are frugal, industrious, orderly, and intelligent. They have a small (Cong.) church and a spacious schoolhouse. They receive their proportion of the common school money, and the school commissioner of the district employs a teacher for them. They are exempt from taxation, and are debarred the exercise of the elected franchise... The Indians annually elect three Trustees, who with the concurrence of 2 justices, can lease certain of their lands to the whites.

Prime (1845)[34] also noted that the Shinnecock were divided into two small communities (Sebbonac Neck and Shinnecock Neck) and were "amalgamated with African blood" totaling thirty families and 140 individuals of all ages.

Controversy

Within the context of this significant cultural and racial transformation of the Shinnecock community, further conflicts between the community and individual members and the town continued. For the Shinnecock, growing usage by town residents of lands available at Shinnecock Hills increased the chances of problems. This arena of potential problems, perhaps another indication of Shinnecock social change, moved into the judicial realm and heralded a significant shift in town-Shinnecock relations.

The Austin Rose v. Luther Bun, James Bun, and Francis Willis Suit

As common lands not being used by Indians under the 1703 lease agreement, in the Shinnecock Hills region of Southampton were either sold or leased to non-Indians by the town proprietors, tensions and problems between the two resident populations increased, especially in the Sebbonac Neck area.

On March 1,1825 the town proprietary trustees of Southampton directed that two of its members begin to "hire out" lands at "Sebonack to town inhabitants for grazing purposes."[35] The trustees continued to do so on a yearly basis. Additionally, it must be remembered that the Shinnecock, under the 1703 lease agreement were required to fence their agricultural tracts from April through September each and every year. From October through the end of the following February, these lands reverted back to a common land status to be used for winter grazing (to be "stinted").

The town trustee records noted that in 1837, Vincent Cuffee, one of the Shinnecock trustees, bought suit against the town trustees over this practice of off-season grazing both at Shinnecock Neck and in the Shinnecock Hills area. No court adjudication of this issue has been located.[36] The same town trustee meeting minutes show that this grazing practice continued through 1848, wherein, Capt John Rose and David Rose were given winter pasture and grazing rights to the same area.[37]

During this same time period (April 1826)[38] it will be recalled that the town trustees had proposed to the Shinnecock to exchange their lands in the Shinnecock Hills region for lands on Shinnecock Neck. Nothing became of that offer.

On April 11, 1843[39] the town trustees, seeking to avert any future grazing or pasturing conflicts on Shinnecock Neck proposed to Luther Cuffee, Wicks Cuffee, and Stephen Walkus, the Shinnecock trustees, that Shinnecock Neck be divided by a fence, "the indians to improve the South Half and the trustees to improve the North half for a term of six years." The offer was accepted by the Shinnecock trustees and during this stipulated time period, no further disputes occurred on Shinnecock Neck. All entry and use of the town's portion of the Neck was strictly controlled by an overseer appointed by the town for that specific purpose, "no person Shall put any Creature in the said Neck until he have Right for the same for the Season" Any infractions were subject to a twelve dollar fine, an excessive amount for that time.

Tensions still remained, with both sides trying to articulate their rights. In April of 1848 a committee of town trustees was appointed to sell and lease the town's common land holdings at "the Sebonack Sedges"[40] surrounding the Shinnecock used lands in that area. The following year (April 13, 1849) a second committee was appointed, "to sell at Discretion the Wood land at Sebonack"[41] The simmering issue between claimed Shinnecock rights and those of the town over the Sebbonac lands came to a head on March 26, 1853. At that time the town trustees passed a resolution as follows,

> Whereas the Proprietor trustees of the town of Southampton have hired the grazing rights on Shinecock Hills to Austin Rose for one year for the sum of Thirty dollars snd whereas it appears that the Indians have allotted a part of said land for the purpose of planting without fencing. Therefore Resolved that the Trustees will defend the said Austin Rose Against any suit brought by Said Indians for trespass on Said land without a sufficient fence, And that the President be impowered to carry the above Resolution into effect and to employ Counsel as he shall think proper.

Differences that in the past had been resolved informally between the town and the Shinnecock via their respective trustees now were to be settled formally in a court of law. Only an incident was needed between Rose and the Shinnecock to force their hands. The previous cooperative relationship was transformed into one of direct confrontation. Austin Rose had received a valid one year grazing lease of proprietary-owned common land from the trustees The Shinnecock used planting rights acquired via the 1703 conditional lease without the required fencing of the planting field that demarcated an allotted use boundary.

On June 17, 1853 a complaint was filed with the Suffolk County Circuit Court[42] by Abraham Rose, an attorney representing Austin Rose, the plaintiff in a complaint against Luther Bun, James Bun and Francis Willis, at that time the Shinnecock trustees. The complaint, in part, read,

> The above plaintiff, being duly sworn says that he is lawfully entitled to the possession of the following personal property claimed within the ---, that is to say, three hundred and twenty sheep and lambs, by virtue of a special property lease which is, that he is in lawfully in possession of a certain tract of land situate within the said town of Southampton known as Shinncock Hills, by virtue of a lease for the same from the Trustees of the Proprietors of the town of Southampton, and so being in the possession of the same as aforesaid he has taken in large quantities of sheep and cattle within the said premises for various individuals to graze and pasture, among which were the aforesaid three hundred and twenty sheep and lambs, that the said sheep and lambs were wrongfully taken by Luther Bun, James Bun and Francis Willis-the above named defendants, and are wrongfully detained from the plaintiff by Ebenezer W. Payne their agent:

> Now the alledged cause of the taking and detention thereof according to the defendants best knowledge information and belief is as follows:

> A pretended trespass of the said sheep and lambs upon certain corn growing upon the said Shinnecock Hills, claimed by

certain Indians of the Shinnecock tribe of Indians, and detained by the said- Luther Bun, James Bun and Francis Willis-the said defendants, on the sixteenth day of June, and delivered by them to the said Ebenezer W. Payne as one the Pound Master of the Town of Southampton...and locked up in the public pound in the village of Southampton....

In his complaint, Rose demanded that the sheep and lambs in his care be returned and that the defendants pay costs and damages amounting to $100.00. On July 18, 1853, the defendants filed an answer to the Court. It read in part,

...That at or before the time mentioned in the said complaint they the said defendants and Stephen Walker, David Bun, Paul Cuffee, Wicks Cuffee, Oliver Kellis, Ann Williams, Darius Jackson, Thomas Beman, Minerva Greeen, Age Cuffee, Charles Killis, Darius See and Charles Smith were lawfully possessed of a certain close piece or parcel of land situate upon Shinnecock Hills in the town of Southampton... and the three hundred and twenty sheep mentioned in the said complaint... were taken as alleged in the complaint were wrongfully upon the said close piece or parcel of land eating and destroying the corn then there growing and doing damage to the said defendants... wherefore the said other persons above named seized and took the said 320 sheep in the said close piece or parcel of land.

The Shinnecock defendants claimed that the sheep and lambs in question should not have been released back to Rose, but to them for the damages the animals did to their crops. Ultimately, the Court ruled in Rose's favor on the basis of the Shinnecock's failure to erect a fence around the parcel that would have kept the sheep out as required by the town. Rose, as a lessee of grazing land, was not required to do so. The Shinnecock were fined a total of $92.00 for damages and costs. The Shinnecock appealed the decision to the State Supreme Court which affirmed the lower court's decision in favor of Rose.

This Court action exposed the continuing problem in the maintenance of the 1703 lease, the co-use of the Shinnecock Hills lands by both the town and the Shinnecock. The issue first arose when Rose and the trustees felt that the Shinnecock did in part, plant on lands that were leased to Rose. The Shinnecock, in turn, believed they were planting on rightful allotted lands, but they failed to follow the requirements to do so.

The Shinnecock were limited to the allotment and use of 125 acres in Shinnecock Hills for planting, along with one square mile for timber harvesting as well as the southern half of Shinnecock Neck and the village sit at Sebbonac Neck. The rest of the lands in the Hills, except those in private fee holding, were proprietary-owned common lands managed by the trustees. Interestingly both sides appeared willing to live with this issue and state of affairs until the matter of the wandering sheep and the significant damage to the Shinnecock's subsistence crops came into play. For the Shinnecock, a significant portion of their subsistence activities was threatened; for Rose, his liability for 320 sheep that were in his care placed him in a difficult position.

Was there a solution to the prevention of such future occurrences?

IX. Resolution

As Prime (c.1845)[1] noted earlier, the Shinnecock were at the time of his writing divided into two communities, Sebbonac Neck and Shinnecock Neck totaling thirty-five families or 140 individuals. French,[2] writing in 1861 noted that these communities had merged into a single acculturated community of twenty dwellings, totaling 200 persons that included its own church and public-financed school and teacher. The members of the Shinnecock community were not considered to be accepted inhabitants of the town, but state wards under the Town's jurisdiction as non-residents. Thus, there property was not taxable nor as a result, did the Shinnecock have the right to vote in Town elections.

During this period of rapid acculturation and racial change, the Shinnecock community learned to use other legal tools that were at their disposal other than face-to-face meetings with the Town trustees to resolve differences. The Shinnecock now utilized not only direct petitions to state authorities, but also the state judicial system to seek redress of perceived wrongs.

Other than learning to use these additional resources, what other factors changed the nature of the relationship between the town and the Shinnecock community? Previously, the Shinnecock addressed their needs to the town proprietary trustees. These proprietary trustees were responsible for town lands not yet sold into private ownership by the proprietors. As the acreage of non-sold lands decreased, especially in the Shinnecock Hills region of Southampton, the proprietary trustees power to influence affairs declined. If a dispute arose between the Shinnecock and a land –owner, the trustees would have no jurisdiction in the matter. As land in fee ownership in

Southampton increased, the effectiveness of the trustees decreased. The political power base within Southampton shifted to two groups, the fee-holding inhabitants of the town and the town justices of the peace. Theses justices were, themselves fee-holding town inhabitants, who, despite the impartial nature of their office, often felt answerable to the town landholders who elected them to their office. This shift in basic town-Shinnecock daily interaction, coupled with increased population pressures created tensions between the two parties of which there was not an effective mediating body. This change exposed internal weaknesses in the 1703 lease agreement.

It will be recalled that earlier, during April of 1826, the proprietary trustees attempted to alleviate these growing tensions by making an offer to the Shinnecock trustees. In that offer, the proprietary trustees offered to "give them all Shinnecock Neck..." if the Shinnecock would "give up to the Proprietors the other Indian land to the use of the said Proprietors...."[3] That is, the town was willing to vest the Shinnecock community with fee-simple land rights to Shinnecock neck, if they would surrender their leasehold rights to lands in the Shinnecock Hills. This offer was not accepted by the Shinnecock.

Thirty-two years later, in 1858, a similar offer was again offered to the Shinnecock community by the trustees. The offer would again offer the Shinnecock community fee-simple title to a land base of its own. In return, proprietary-owned unsold lands within the Shinnecock Hills region of Southampton would be freed to supply the demands of a growing town population. To this end, in April of 1855, the town proprietors directed that a committee be formed to sell the remaining common lands "from Water Mill to Canoe Place."[4] This directive included the remaining unsold proprietary lands in Shinnecock Hills. At a proprietors trustee meeting held on December 23, 1858[5] it was noted,

> ...the Committee appointed at the last meeting, to confer with the Indians and to agree with them as to a Division-reported as follows- They have made a bargain with the said Indians- by which the Proprietors are to convey to the Indians the Neck (Shinecock and the Indians are to release to the proprietors the residue of the Indian lands...The Indians are to have the lower string of fence across the Neck and One half of the upper string now stranding & deviding the Neck from the Hills....

Shinnecock Neck was still unsold, proprietary owned common land. This time the offer of a land exchange offered by the proprietors was accepted by a majority of eligible Shinnecock community membership. It was to be the proprietary trustees last effective interaction with the Shinnecock.

A Land of their Own

In order to ensure the legitimacy of this land exchange, it was agreed by both parties to formally request both the sanction of this action, and consent of the New York State legislature. On January 7, 1859, the following petition was submitted by the twenty-one undersigned Shinnecock community members that included all three Shinnecock trustees, David Bun, Stephen Walker, and Wickham Cuffee,

> To the Legislature of the State of New York:

> The petition of the undersigned persons belonging to the Shinnecock tribe of Indians, residing in the town of Southampton, county of Suffolk, respectfully showeth:

> ...Your petitioners further show that of late years various disputes have arisen between the said Indians and the trustees of the proprietors of common lands of the town of Southampton in regard to their respective rights under the

several deeds and leases, and that to put an end to these differences they have consented to an arrangement with the said trustees by which they are to surrender their lease to certain portion of these lands, and the trustees are to reconvey to the said tribe the residue; and further your petitioners are informed and believe that the said bargain and arrangement cannot be consummated unless by the consent of the legislature; they would therefore most respectfully ask the legislature to pass a law for this purpose, as your petitioners will ever pray.

James L. Cuffee
Wicks Cuffee
David S. Bun
Age Cuffee
John Thompson
Davis Jacobson
Afphonso Boardman
Wm. Richard
Tobias Cole
Stephen Walker
James L. Cuffee

James Lee
Saira H. Walker
Paul Cuffee
Luther Cuffee
Vincent Cuffee
Addison J. Ryer
Charles Kellis
Wickham Cuffee
Joel Davis
Thomas Beaman

I certify that the above names were signed in my presence

Albert J. Post
Clerk of Southampton[6]

The action undertaken by the Shinnecock community was not without dissent from some community members. Some twelve community members submitted an undated counter-petition alleging that the January 7, 1859 document contained forged signatures, despite the attesting signature of the Southampton town clerk that all the petitioners signed the document in his presence.[7]

We, the undersigned affiants, on oath depose and say:

That we are members of the Shinnecock Tribe of Indians of Southampton, in said county of Suffolk; that we have submitted to us the names of the signers to a certain petition which was presented to the assembly of New York State by certain people claiming to be Shinnecock Indians., residing in said county of Suffolk in 1859,and presented to the assembly on January 7th, 1859; and we depose that said names, as signed thereon is said petition, were forgeries, and of this we are ready to offer substantial and conclusive evidence in any Court of law...

David Killes	Fannie Ashman
A. H. Cuffee	Lydia Ward
Anna C. Kellis	Harriet Richards.
James L. Cuffee	Mary J. Walker
Mary Brewer	N. J. Cuffee
Chas. H. Ashman	Maria Cuffee

The State Legislature decided otherwise and on March 6, 1859 passed legislation[8] affirming and consenting to the land exchange,

Whereas, the Shinnecock tribe of Indians, by virtue of a lease for one thousand years, are in the occupation of a tract of land lying in the town of Southampton, in the county of Suffolk, called Shinnecock Neck, and are living therein as a tribe, subject to certain rights of pasturage and the fee of the said land is in the trustees of the proprietors of the common and undivided lands and marshes in the town of Southampton, and other lands are held in the same manner; and whereas, the rights of the said tribe of Indians and said trustees of said proprietors are of such a nature as to be conflicting, and have become the cause of frequent and expensive litigation, and render the improvement of the land far less valuable than the same would be if equitably divided and improved in severalty; and whereas, a verbal agreement and arrangement has been entered into between the said tribe of Indians and said trustees of said proprietors for the full and clear release, each to the other, of all their rights on either side of an established and well defined line, to the end that each may improve and own in severalty all the land on their side of said line, to the end that each may improve and own in severalty all the land on their side of the line. Now therefore:

The People of the State of New York, represented in Senate and Assembly, do enact the as follows:

Section 1. The trustees of the said tribe of Indians are hereby authorized and empowered, in behalf of said Indians, to convey, release and quit-claim to the trustees of the said proprietors of common and undivided lands and marshes in the town of Southampton, by deed in the ordinary form, all their right, title and interesting and to certain lands in the town of Southampton, by deed in the ordinary form, and to be acknowledged in the usual manner before the county judge of Suffolk county, all their right, title, and interest in and to certain lands in the town of Southampton, Suffolk county generally known as Shinnecock Hills, and Sebonnack Neck, and lying north of a certain line commencing at the head of the creek and running along the Indian ditch, where the fence now stands, to the the Stephen Post meadow, so called, thence along the old ditch on the South side of the said meadow to old fort pond, where the water fence formerly stood. And the said trustees of the said proprietors are hereby authorized to receive the same in consideration of a deed in like manner, in the ordinary form, and to acknowledged in the usual manner before the county judge of Suffolk county, conveying, confirming, and releasing to the said trustees of the said Indians, in behalf of the said Shinnecock tribe, all that tract of land commonly called Shinnecock Neck, and lying south of the before described line, commencing at the head of the creek on the east side of the Neck, and running along the Indian ditch, where the fence now stands, to the Stephen Post meadow, so called; thence along the old ditch on the south side of the said meadow to old Fort Pond, where the water fence former stood.

2. The true intent and meaning of this act is, and it shall be construed to be, to enable the said Shinnecock tribe of Indians to exchange all their rights in and to the land north of said line, for full release to them by said trustees of said proprietors, of all their rights in and to all land south of said line; and the consent of the people of the state of New York is hereby granted to such exchange.

3. This act shall take effect immediately.

On April 21, 1859, an exchange of lands between the town proprietors and the Shinnecock trustees took place.[9] The Shinnecock received a "Transfer of Title in Fee Simple..." to all the lands of Shinnecock Neck south of the "Indian ditch" signed by all thirteen members "as said Trustees of said Proprietors..."[10] What is important to note was that this action was, as the State of New York noted, to, " exchange certain rights in land." Section two of the State's enabling legislation affirmed this. No mention was made of establishing an Indian reservation for the Shinnecock. The clear intent was that the Shinnecock, as a cooperate entity, was to assume fee simple ownership to lands of Shinnecock Neck. The State did not declare the Neck to be a reservation nor did the state assume any trust or fiduciary responsibilities over this land. The only state-recognized governance over the lands of Shinnecock Neck was that of the Shinnecock trustees by virtue of the 1792 legislative enactment. In turn, the Shinnecock trustees released the town proprietors from all the stipulations and conditions contained in the 1703 lease agreement.

During this period, that is, the latter half of the 19th century, acculturation to the main or dominant culture had racially, socially, and ideologically transformed the Shinnecock community. By 1861 they no longer spoke their aboriginal language. As a result, oral tradition, long an important component of Indian society, became dysfunctional by the influx of anglicized African Americans, who spoke a different language (English) and had assimilated a different cultural tradition (Christian/European), that of the dominant culture.

At a "Special meeting of the Proprietor Trustees," held on January 8, 1861,[11] it was resolved to sell all the unsold lands at Sebbonac Neck and Shinnecock Hills at public auction. These lands were so-acquired by the Long Island Improvement Company.

X. The Western Lands and the Shinnecock

With the completion of the 1859 land exchange all existing Indian land rights east of Canoe Place were extinguished, save those newly fee title rights acquired for Shinnecock Neck by the Shinnecock trustees. One would have expected that this exchange would have resulted in the end of land-related conflict between the town of Southampton and the Shinnecock community. Such was not to be.

More Litigation: The Lands at Canoe Place

The era of litigation, rather than accommodation and compromise, continued. The 1859 Bun suit was only the beginning of a string of suits bought by the Shinnecock through 1919. The nature of the suits changed. No longer was litigation directed towards the town of Southampton per se, now the emphasis was upon individuals who were deemed to have wronged the Shinnecock community. Unfortunately, these suits were bought on the basis of ignorance of historical facts by the Shinnecock trustees and adjudicated by jurists lacking a similar historical knowledge of the foundational facts of the suits presented to them. These suits will be examined in detail below.

The next area of Shinnecock-town interaction concerned the lands west of the present-day Canoe Place canal in Southampton. This was the last area to be disposed of by the proprietors, and the last to experience settlement. Historically, the Shinnecock never had any significant village or settlement locations in this region except for a winter village in the present day Southampton village of Quag. Quag bordered on the present-day town of Brookhaven. Archaeological excavations support this historical finding.[1] The historic Shinnecock utilized these lands for hunting and fishing, both of which were present in abundance. By the advent of the twentieth century the town was utilizing these Canoe Place lands for residential growth as well as a continued timber resource, for both domestic and commercial use.

"to draw their Lots in Conew place Division": The Survey and Division of 1738

The town of Southampton anticipating future timber requirements, did, as early as 1737, turn to these former Ogden/Topping purchase lands west of Canoe Place as a source of timber resources. The town's proprietors, as the successors by either inheritance or by purchase of the original town 1639/1640 patentees or "undertakers," had the right to allot land among themselves and to issue outright grants of land. Town records and other period historical writings and documents tell us that these allotments were of two types[2]. First there was the home lot allotment which conferred the right of fee ownership to the allottee. Second was the allotment to commonage rights, that is, the right of access to natural resources within the town. No fee was transferred in connection with commonage rights, as these lands remained under the ownership of the proprietors. What was allotted was an equable access by the proprietors to natural resources, such as timber or meadows that were held in common for the exclusive use by the proprietors.

In 1738 the town trustees appointed a committee to lay out lots within a newly-executed division known as the Canoe ("Canew") Place Division, running from Canoe Place to Red Creek, east to west, and from Peconic Bay to the "Country" (or "Quag") Road at Tianah (the present-day Montauk Highway), north to south. They did so and reported their work to the town trustees in a report dated March 27, 1738.[3] The Committee left the Peconic Bay shoreline beaches to the low water mark undivided and remanded its continued ownership to the proprietors of Southampton in order to ensure equable access to seashore resources. Their use was regulated by the town trustees.

Following the laying out of the Canoe Place Division in 1738, on April 2, 1739, the town proprietors allotted the 39 lots of the Canoe Place Division amongst themselves, by drawing lots. For example,[4]

> Southampton April 2, 1739: the propriatours of said town being legally warned by the constable to meet together in order to draw their Lots in Conew place Division in quaga purchase, and the said propriatours being convened together in the meeting house on sd day in presence of Abram Cooper and Hugh Gelston justices, did prosede to draw their lots in the following way & manner, (vis)
>
> | Lot No | | |
> |---|---|---|
> | 1 | Ephraim White | 2 fifties |
> | | Hezekiah Topping | 1 fifty |
> | | Jeremiah Jagger | 1 fifty |
> | | Samuel Jagger | 1 fifty |
> | | Benjamin Jagger | 1/2 fifty |
> | | Nathaniel Howell | 1/2 fifty |
> | 3 | Mathias Burnet | 1-1/2 fifty |
> | | John Mitchell | 1-1/2 fifty |
> | 4 | Matthew Wood & Brother | 7/8 fifty |
> | | Ephraim Hildreth | 1/4 fifty |
> | | Daniel Sayre | 1/2 & 1/8 fifty |
> | | Widow Mary Howell & son | 1/2 fifty |
> | | Elas Pelletrue | 1/8 fifty |
> | | Theeophilus Pierson | 1/8 fifty |
> | | John Reves.... | 1/2 fifty.... |

These 39 lots were not initially intended to be fee-held home lots for the future allottees. Instead, these lands constituted the town's timber reserve. A "fifty" represents an amount of pine and oak timber to the value of fifty pounds Sterling. No value was placed upon the land itself. The lots were not intended to be occupied but were intended to be allotted for wood-cutting rights or commonage only. The 1739 allotment of woodlots in the Canoe Place Division were for usufructuary privilege of common resources (commonage), not outright fee ownership. Simply put, commonage in colonial society implied a right to usage in common, not right of ownership in private, a town's common being an example. The English word "commoner" was a term initially used to denote one who belonged to the proprietary class, and who by virtue of this standing, had a right to commonage thus becoming a "commoner."

From the time of the 1739 allotment of rights in the Canoe Place Division through the time of the American Revolution, there was limited land conveyance related activity within the Canoe Place Division. Additionally, a road, "Squires Road," (also known as "Cordwood Road") was laid out and constructed in 1795 following in part a pre-existing path crossing through the Canoe Place Division lands from Red Creek to the Canoe Place.[5]

The Shinnecock's involvement with these lands began as a result of over harvesting of the timber resources as leased to them by the town in the Shinnecock Hills region. It involved a portion of the Canoe Place Division known as "Westwoods."[6] This parcel abutted Peconic Bay on the north, the present-day Canoe Place Canal (historically the "Canoe Place pond" or "ditch" and later the "Newtown Pond") on the east. Canoe Place pond also served as the boundary between Canoe Place and the Shinnecock Hills region of Southampton. The present-day Montauk Highway ("Country Road" or "Quag Road") was Westwoods' southern boundary. Westwoods was bisected by a road, established in 1795, the "Cordwood Road, and later, "Squires Road."

In the July 1859 court suit cited earlier (Luther Bunn & Others v The Trustees of the Proprietors of the Town of Southampton) Bunn, a Shinnecock trustee, noted,[7]

> That there is no timber upon the leased premises and there was very little there fifty years ago [circa 1809]

The lack of available timber in 1809 helps to put into context comments made by James H. Foster, a Southampton native familiar with the Shinnecock during the 1888 New York Special Committee hearings:[8]

> Q. Do they claim any other land on the Island? A. They also claim to own a tract of woods in this town about five miles from here.
> Q. About five miles away? A. Yes, sir; in the town, about fifty acres.
> Q. Upon what is that claim based? A. Through the tribe purchasing it seventy or eighty years ago.
> Q. How long did they hold it? A. They held it up to four or five years ago.
> Q. And still claim it? A. They still claim to own it.
> Q. How much is there in this tract which they claim? A. About fifty acres.[9]
> Q. Are they in possession of this land now? A. They were up until four or five years ago; they cut wood from it.

The lands being referenced to in this testimony included a portion of Westwoods, specifically the upper portions of the surveyed lots: the Blank Lot through Lot #3. The Shinnecock claimed they purchased the land, but possessed no deed of conveyance. As noted earlier, the Legislative Act of February 24, 1792 did not empower the Shinnecock trustees to make land purchases. Their powers were legislatively limited to land allotments. They claimed that they purchased the land from a townsman named Wakeman Foster.[10]

As it turned out, Wakeman Foster, despite the Shinnecock's claims to the contrary, never owned any land in this area. Foster owned land further south near the present-day Canoe Place Inn (circa 1801) on the Montauk Highway.

Foster's reference that the lands were purchased "seventy or eighty years ago" would mean that the Shinnecock purchased land in Westwoods about 1808, as reflected in the historical record of an Indian Trustee meeting held on April 7, 1808. As reflected in the historical record of this April 7, 1808 meeting, this acquisition was actually a decision by the Indian trustees to obtain a lease of 120 acres in the Westwoods area,[11]

> At an Indian trustee Meeting held on the 7th Day of April 1808.
> Proceeded as folweth
> Voted that they, by order of Rogers & Caleb Cooper Esquires, & James Bun and Aaron Cuffee Indian trustees---
> Voted that they lease 120 Acres in the field which they are to enclose on the *North Side of the Road from Conklin's Corner to extend East to the Old field,* by order of Rogers & Caleb Cooper Esquires, & James Bun and Aaron Cuffee Indian trustees—(emphasis added)

The "road" referred to in these minutes was Squires Road. The corner was the southwest corner of Lot #2. Here a corner was formed by lands belonging to Israel Conklin. He owned lot #3 to the shoreline of Peconic Bay. He also owned Lots #2 and #1 north to Squires Road. The intersection of Lot #3 with the northerly boundary of Conklin's land in Lot #2 at the Squires Road formed a corner. In addition Conklin now owned the Blank Lot in its entirety. According to the trustees' description, the land had to be to the East of Conklin's corner. This ruled out the southeast corner formed by Lot #1 at Squires Road and the Blank Lot because there were no open eastward lands available in that direction.

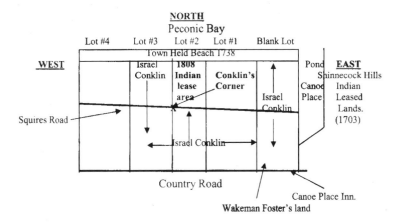

An examination of the April 22, 1807 Indian trustee meeting minutes clearly shows that the availability of growing or plowing land was not an issue within the Shinnecock 1703 leased lands. Comments made in the own trustee records of April 14, 1793, April 28, 1794, April 19, 1798, and April 22, 1807 bear fact out. Thus, it would appear that the April 1808 vote was made to authorize the leasing of additional timber land from the town proprietors to the Shinnecock.

Apparently the Shinnecock trustees' lease from the town of Southampton was for land in these erstwhile vacant Topping/Canoe Place purchase lands. This leased "Westwoods" parcel was to become the subject of intense litigation between the town and the Shinnecock in 1890, 1919, and again in 2005.

At the root of this problem was the mistaken belief by the Shinnecock trustees that they owned the property in Westwoods in fee simple. This belief may have been the result of the significant socio-cultural change that had occurred within the Shinnecock community. During this period the Shinnecock, like the Mashpee of Cape Cod in Massachusetts, the Eastern and Mashantucket Pequot of Connecticut, the

Narragansett of Rhode Island, and the neighboring Poospatuck on Long Island, had transitioned from a predominately Native American community to one that became predominantly Black.[12] Within this transformational process cultural norms and practices were either replaced or transformed. With the loss of the native language, memories based upon oral tradition, an essential element for the transmittal of cultural and historical knowledge within Indian social groups, became distorted. Leased lands became "purchased lands"; "woodlots" became "occupied lands."

In 1885, believing themselves to be in fee ownership of the Westwoods parcel, the Shinnecock trustees attempted to sell the land to one Miles Carpenter for 100 dollars. Carpenter at the time was the owner of the still-existent Canoe Place Inn. Similarly, earlier, in January of 1873, the Shinnecock, believing themselves to be owners of the Peconic Bay beach lands, attempted to sell this beach shoreline to Elisha King on October 10, 1857, not realizing or recognizing that the proprietors had reserved the beach to themselves in 1738.[13] Thus the following conveyance,[14]

> Made this Twenty first day of January in the year one thousand eight hundred and Seventy Three, Between David W. Bunns, Oliver J. Nellis and John Walker all duly Elected Trustees of the Shinecock Tribe of Indians residing in the town of Southampton County of Suffolk and State of New York parties of the first part and Elisha King of the Town, County, and State aforesaid party of the second part. Witnesseth that the said parties of the first part and in consideration of the sum of forty dollars to them duly paid before the delivery hereof have bargained and sold and by these presents do grant and convey to the said party of the second part his heirs and assigns forever all of a certain beach or sandy shore lying in the town of Southampton aforesaid and north of the village of Canoe Place and bounded to the West by the lands of William W. Warner and the North by

Peconic Bay on the East by the lands of proprietors of Shinnecock Hills and on the South in part by lands of Barnabas Hubbard the width of beach from Said Hubbard's land to the [ ] [ ]Bay being about thirty four rods and in part by the Pond known as Newtown pond and in part by the Cleff of the land of the Shinnecok Indians as shown in the following plot Subject to any legally constituted highways

This conveyance, included a survey drawing of the purchase as depicted below.

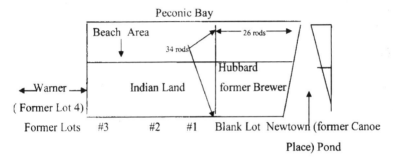

Former Reeves & Macke//Barnabas Hubbard lands

The Shinnecock trustees claimed the northern portion of the former Blank Lot as well as the northernmost portions of Lots 1-3 to a depth of 34 rods from the beach. Lot 4 was owned by a man named Warner. The Shinnecock, of course, had no right to sell any beach lands. These lands along the Peconic Bay shoreline, as mentioned earlier had been reserved to the town in the 1738 Canoe Place Division.

Any ownership claims made by the Shinnecock trustees to the lands westward from Newtown Pond to the boundary line for Lots #3-4 were equally invalid. All three lots were town-owned woodlots laid out in 1738. The land adjacent to the pond and shoreline constituted the former "Blank Lot" that was acquired in fee from the proprietary trustees by one Jeremiah Culver in 1738. Both this lot and portions of upper

Lot #1 were later held in fee simple by Israel Conklin, Joseph Thompson and Daniel Brewer. The former shoreline lands of Lot#3 were also claimed by the Shinnecock in the King conveyance. It is known that in 1835 the upper portion of lot #3 was in the possession of Edward Reeve and Peter Mackie.

This claim was made despite abundant available documentation demonstrating that these lands and beach had been in continuous private and/or town ownership for over 200 years. The trustees evidently wanted to believe what they perceived to be the truth of the matter, rather than checking the facts.

The 1890 Tribal Trustees v. Cassady Suit

On February 9, 1889 Alphonso Eleazer, Freedland Ryer, and Milton Beamon in their capacity as trustees of the Shinnecock community brought suit against one James Cassady in the Suffolk County Justice Court.[15] The trustees suit complained,

> That on the 14th day of January 1889 the defendant unlawfully and willfully entered with a team of horses and wagon upon land belonging to said Tribe of Indians situate at Canoe Place in said Town of Southampton and carted away wood from said land belonging to said Tribe of Indians of the value of twenty five dollars.

This complaint was later amended (no date provided) to include Charles W. Conklin as a second defendant. Cassady in his defendant's response noted that he had cut the wood under a license given to him by Miles Carpenter who had purchased 100 acres of land at Westwoods from two Shinnecock trustees in 1885 for 100 dollars.[16] Carpenter had died in April of 1890. Was this really land that the Shinnecock owned in fee or did it involve a simple lease? What was the actual extent of the land to which the Shinnecock had any rights to as derived from the 1808 lease?

To begin with, at a Shinnecock trustee meeting held on September 8, 1884,[17] the trustees agreed to lease out twenty acres, "hire but 20 acres of land at Newtown." At their April 9, 1885[18] meeting the trustees, "Resolved that the three trustees go and see Mr. Carpenter about the wood land and find out whether he has bought it or not and report the same…" The trustees noted in their meeting minutes of April 21, 1885[19] that "Mr Carpenter said that he had bought the wood land he did not have a deed but a written agreement between him and the trustees which was as good as a deed." The record goes on to state that one of the trustees, Alphonso Elezar, "said he asked Mr. Carpenter if he had paid Atty Petty any money and the answer was, that you must ask Mr Petty." At their November 9, 1885 meeting[20] the trustees were informed of "the report on Mr. Carpenter, about the woodland which was read from lawyer Benjamin stating, that that sale of the woodland was null & void." In the following entry, the trustees "Voted that the tribe defend any one who might be sued for cutting wood in the west woods." Evidently Carpenter was contesting the actions of the Shinnecock trustees in voiding their sale to him as indicated by an entry in their January 1, 1886 meeting minutes,[21] "Voted that Mr Hudson give his idea of the case on selling of the wood land.…" Evidently the Shinnecock were concerned that Carpenter might have one of their own arrested if they attempted to cut wood on the Westwoods parcel. The bottom line here was that a resolution to lease twenty acres in Westwoods (which amounted to a sub-lease) morphed into an outright sale (the Shinnecock had only the 1808 leasehold rights to the Westwoods parcel) to Carpenter. The Shinnecocks' legal counsel, aware of this problem informed his clients that the sale was "null & void" on the basis that the Shinnecock did not have fee title to the land to convey, and that the trustees were not, under the state statues, allowed to sell or purchase land. Carpenter claimed he had a valid conveyance document.

As a result, the defendants, Cassady and Conklin, asserted the woodlot did not "belong" to the Shinnecock on the basis that the Shinnecock did not have possession of the woodlot in question, nor had they for the previous twenty-five years (circa 1865). The Shinnecock, in part echoing their 1888 Commission testimony, claimed that they had purchased "many years ago" a tract of woodland consisting of 75 acres as opposed to the 50 acres claimed by Mr. Lee in his 1888 testimony to the Special Commission. No supporting deed of conveyance was presented by the Shinnecock to the Court. The facts were clearly in the defendant's favor.

On July 19, 1890 the presiding judge, Willard Bartlett, determined:

> That the tribe of Shinnecock Indians have been in quiet and peaceable possession of the premises, where the alleged trespass occurred for upward of sixty years [1830].

Additionally, Judge Bartlett made the determination that an enabling state legislative act had to be passed authorizing such a sale. He did so on the precedent set by the 1859 Act enabling the Shinnecock Neck- Shinnecock Hills land exchange. Thus, in his opinion the Shinnecock's sale of the Westwoods parcel and Carpenter's purchase were invalid. Judge Bartlett did not address the issue whether the Shinnecock had a valid ownership claim to begin with. Carpenters claim, which was the foundational issue of this dispute remained unresolved. Judge Bartlett's decision was a gross error due to the lack of diligent research into the issue before the court.

What does the historical record tell us? As demonstrated earlier, the town of Southampton had acquired all right, title, and interest to the lands of the Canoe Place Division within the Topping Purchase more than 200 years earlier. All these lands were divided and allotted as woodlots (except the Blank Lot lands of Jeremiah Culver). In their 1873 conveyance to Elisha King,[22] the Shinnecock trustees laid out the lands they considered to be theirs within the Canoe Place Division,

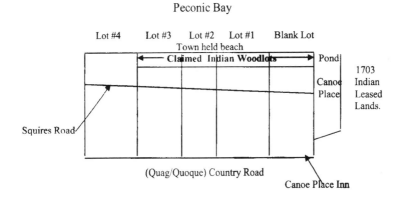

As depicted in the 1873 document purporting to convey to Elisha King, the Shinnecock trustees claimed lands abutting westerly on the eastern boundary of Lot #4 owned by William Warner eastward to the Canoe Place (Newton) Pond. They also claimed lands south from Peconic Bay to a depth of 34 rods or 561 feet, just a fraction of the depth of Westwoods claimed by the Shinnecock.

The Blank Lot abutting Canoe Place was conveyed by the town proprietors to Jeremiah Culver circa 1738,

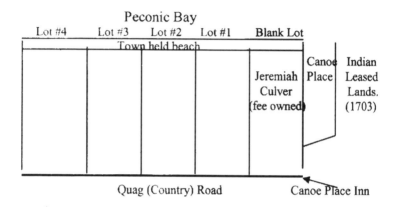

1738 Town Woodlot Division Survey[23]

The beach area was reserved to the Town of Southampton,

we left all the beach from Canew Place pond on the north side to Reed crick gut undivided from high water mark to low water mark for the use of the proprietors to get and cart stone to pass and repass from time to time and all times hereafter...And then we proseded to survey all the land between the aforesaid beach and highway from Jeremiah Culver land, which he bought of the owners of said Purchase...

This document negates the right of the Shinnecock to the beach land along Peconic Bay and their claim to the northern portion of the Blank Lot abutting Canoe Place Pond as well as the Bay shoreline as made in the Elisha King conveyance.

By 1805 Israel Conklin had acquired not only the Blank Lot from Jeremiah Culver, but also Lots #1 and #2 northward to Squires Road. He had also acquired Lot #3 to Peconic Bay. Lot #4 was owned by Moses Culver.

As noted earlier, the ownership of first four lots of the Canoe Place Division as of 1804 was as follows,[24]

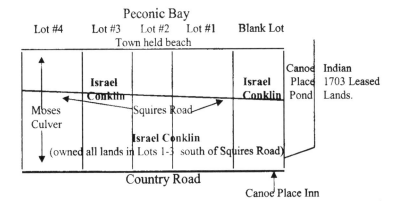

By 1848 Conklin had acquired lands north of Squires Road in Lots #1 and #2. Reeves and Mackie had acquired Conklin's former lands in the northern portion of Lot #3 and Wells had acquired a portion of Lot #1 abutting the Peconic Bay shoreline. Thus the various claims of the Shinnecock to Lots #3, the Blank Lot, and Lot #1 on the coastline are unfounded

As of 1847 ownership of the first four lots of the Canoe Place Division was as follows,[25]

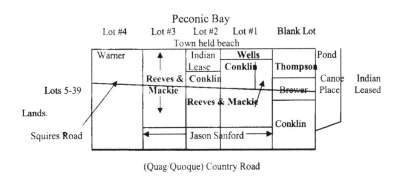

The historical record clearly demonstrates that the Shinnecock were using only the northern portion of Lot #2 abutting the town-owned coastline beach for woodcutting purposes under the 1808 lease from the town proprietors. The Conklin parcel occupying portions of Lots #1 and #2 was bounded easterly by the lands of Mackie and Reeves, northerly and westerly by "Indian land." A tract of land owned by Thomas and Martin Wells occupied the northern portion of Lot#1 to the beach.[26] Their land is mentioned as abutting north of the lands owned by Israel and Cornelia Conklin. It spanned the entire width of Lot #1. By 1857 the adjoining Thompson lands were owned by Barnabas Hubbard.[27]

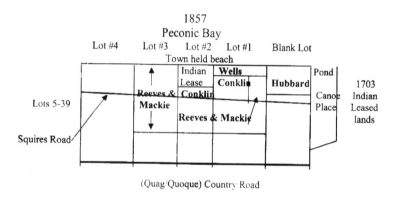

In the final analysis, Judge Barlett's primary and dubious rationale for his decision in Shinnecock Trustees v. Cassady was simply:

> The position of this tract of woodland with reference to the reservation on which the Indians live is analogous to that of a wood-lot belonging to an improved farm; and it seems to me that the evidence of possession is therefore sufficient...No deed to the Tribe or the trustees is produced, nor is it pretended that any is known to exist.

One of the glaring errors in this analogy is the fact that the settlement at Shinnecock Neck was approximately six miles from the woodlot in question. Thus, the woodlot was not in an analogous proximity to Shinnecock Neck. Thus, the basic premise of Judge Bartlett's decision is in error. Moreover, the decision reveals no consideration of the historical documentation referenced herein which demonstrate the true nature and extent of the Shinnecock's leasehold rights in Westwoods. Clearly, the leasehold area in Westwoods was of much smaller dimensions than the Shinnecock trustees imagined.

The 1919 Shinnecock Tribe v. Hubbard Suit

In contrast to the 1890 "Tribal Trustees v Cassady" suit during which the Shinnecock laid claim to ownership of 75 acres of woodland at Westwoods, the Shinnecock trustees now claimed in this 1919 suit that their Westwoods parcel consisted of 100 acres. Once again, the Shinnecock were unable to introduce any documentary evidence of their claim of ownership, and were relegated to a claim that they held title by adverse possession, by virtue of simple occupation by at least "four or five families of said tribe" for a period of at least 70 years (1849) prior to the suit. No such proof of occupation was proffered. Additionally, testimony given by Mr. Foster during the 1888 hearings also argues against such claims. In his testimony he noted that the Shinnecock had not cut wood on their purported lands for five years previous to the hearing, lands and that the land there was "rough, hilly and mostly sandy and fit for nothing but a wood lot..."[28]

Inconsistency was also present within the Shinnecock's complaint. In their initial complaint (May 1, 1919) the Shinnecock plaintiffs claimed that they sold and delivered 1,235 cubic feet of loam to the defendant who, according to the plaintiffs, refused to pay for it. Yet, in the October 9, 1922 judgment, the Shinnecock trustees claimed 1,689 cubic feet of loam was involved and had significantly changed their facts, now claiming that town employees entered upon their land without their authorization and removed the loam in question.

In staking their claim to 100 aces in the Westwoods area, the Shinnecock also provided boundaries for what they claimed were their lands for the past 70 years,

> Bounded North by Peconic Bay, East by Xtopher Holzman, South by land formerly of Mr. Buchmuller, West by land of Mr. Hardy...
> About 100 acres.

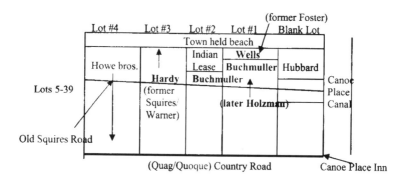

The Hardy lands bordering on the western side of the "Indian land" were those formerly belonging to Samuel Squires.[29] This Hardy property was located in Canoe Place Division Lot #3 bounded northerly by Peconic Bay, and easterly "by the Indian land so-called." The eastern boundary line of this conveyance was 882 feet in length abutting southerly on Newtown Road, a road constructed by the town in 1870 that runs laterally across Westwoods and then due south. Newtown Road was a distance north of the now unused Squires Road. This eastern boundary of the Hardy property conformed to earlier boundary abutment descriptions that confined the Shinnecock woodlot lands to the northern portion of Lot #2 bordering on the beach. A second Hardy parcel abutted this property south of Newtown Road. The eastern boundary of this lower Hardy parcel was abutted easterly by the lands belonging to the heirs of David W. Smith.

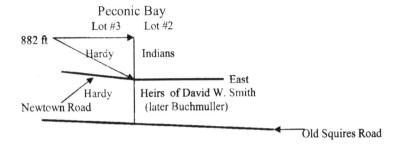

The lands on the eastern side of the Smith heirs' lands were those (10 acres) belonging to Ernest A. Buchmuller.[30] Bordering north on Buchmuller's land were "Indian lands." Bordering southerly on this ten acre parcel was Squires Road. This tells us that the Shinnecock lease parcel was confined to the north side of Newtown Road. In 1909 Buchmuller acquired a 12 acre parcel from Edward Hardy. The western abutment of this former Hardy land was described as "the Indian land." The land abutted easterly on lands belonging to Barabas Hubbard. This parcel was bounded northerly on lands belonging to Richard Wells.[31] Wells acquired this six acre parcel in July of 1858.[32] Wells' northern boundary was on Peconic Bay, east on the Canoe Place Canal, and west on "lands belonging to said Shinnecock Indians."

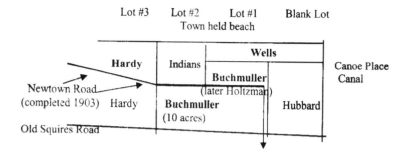

The western boundary of the Indian lands in Lot #2 was, on the basis of the Squires survey of January 1904, 882 feet. In addition we have the eastern side survey of the Indian land boundary given in the purported 1873 Elisha King conveyance[33] of 34 rods or 561 feet. An October 12, 1921 survey conducted by a civil engineer named J.A.S. Gregg of Newtown Road gave a frontage measurement of 2,362.3 lineal feet of the "Old Road through the land leased to Indians":

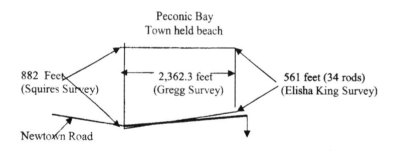

These dimensions as formed by the above abutment analysis and the data contained in the Elisha King deed and Gregg survey created a trapezoid shaped lot that was the Shinnecock's leased land with Newton Road as its southern boundary.

Based on the documents presented above, the data demonstrates that the Indian leased lands located north of

Newtown Road bounding upon Peconic Bay could not have comprised 100 acres. This area actually encompassed only 40.7 acres.[34] The properties described in the Hubbard case as adjoining the so called "Indian Lands" demonstrate that these Indian lands were confined to an area north of Newtown Road and could not have allowed for such acreage.

This parcel (circa 1909) was bounded easterly by Hardy's lands, southerly by Buchmullers' lands formerly those of Smith, Conklin, and Reeves and Mackie and easterly by Buchmullers' and Wells' lands. Buckmullers' land was also north of the now-abandoned Squires Road. This historical record also fails to support later Shinnecock claims to any lands south of Newtown Road.

Most importantly, it must be recalled that the Shinnecock had leased this common land in 1808. If this lease followed the precedent set by the 1747 100-year timber lease, this lease would have been in effect until at least 1908.

The records of the Hubbard case give no indication that the Court was aware of this lease or the history of the Shinnecock's leases of town-owned lands such as Westwoods (e.g., the 1703 lease and the subsequent 1744 and 1747 woodlot leases.) The data also shows that the Shinnecock, in their various suits against individuals or the town over this land, consistently and grossly overstated the acreage of the timber lands they utilized. Inconsistency has been the hallmark of the litigation initiated by the Shinnecock community concerning their purported interest in Westwoods. They claimed they owned the lands at Westwoods in fee, they were lease-holders; they claimed they purchased the Westwood parcel, they declared they held the land by adverse possession; they claimed they owned 50 acres, then they owned 75 acres, then again claimed 100 acres; they claimed they were paid 700 dollars for the Westwood lands by Carpenter when they succeeded in their suit, they were in actuality paid 100 dollars. What was going on here? Why was there such a disparity in claims? These were not dishonest people.

The eminent historian, Bernard Lewis asserted there were three kinds of history of a people: "Remembered," "Recovered," and "Invented."[35] In his book Lewis noted "critical [recovered] history begins with a dissatisfaction with memory and a desire to remedy its deficiencies." Invention on the other hand passes over recovered history and resorts to the "embellishment" of the past, which Lewis noted, "influences inscriptions and chronicles, monographs and textbooks, and all the other media used to project an image and present a case." In the Shinnecock's situation, remembered history failed them. In response they invented it. Tradition and fact were at variance.

On a larger scale, these events are representative of a community that had lost its past and the knowledge of its historical relationship to lands and their neighbors. Simply they perceived their past, not on the basis of facts, but what they wanted it to be. Such an occurrence is not uncommon amongst populations that have been subject to such pronounced socio-cultural change, loss of traditional culture, language, oral tradition, and traditional forms of leadership. Perhaps the most significant factor that altered the Shinnecock's relationship with the town of Southampton was the declining importance of and subsequent dissolution of the proprietary trustees in 1890. For over two centuries the main source of contact, assistance, dispute mediation, and ultimately conflict resolution was through this group of individuals. From 1792 on, it was a personal trustee to trustee relationship. Perhaps of equal importance was the final localization of the Shinnecock community on Shinnecock Neck. In its aftermath both the town trustees and the

Shinnecock became irreverent to Southampton's affairs. This act removed the primary source of friction between the Shinnecock community and the town of Southampton. From that point onwards Shinnecock disputes and subsequent litigation was with individual townsmen, no longer with a corporate entity.

In sum, not only did the Shinnecock as a people and community change, so did the nature of their relationship with whom they coexisted. For their neighbors, their "ancient & Loving ffriends," were changing too.

Notes

Introduction

[1] In particular see: Stone, Gaynell, ed., 1983, "The Shinnecock Indians: A Culture History," *Readings in Long Island Archaeology and Ethnohistory*, Volume VI, Suffolk County Archaeological Association: 1, 37, 54-55, 61-62

Chapter I

[1] Commanger, Henry. ed., 1944 *Documents of American History:* 5, New York, Appelton-Century-Crofts
[2] Williamson, James A. ed. 1962; *The Cabot Voyages and Bristol Discovery under Henry VII*, Hakluyt Society Publications 2nd series CXX: 204-205, London
[3] Curtis E. 1938, *A History of Medieval Ireland 1086-1513*: 38
[4] Commanger 1944: 6
[5] Jennings, Francis, 1975, *The Invasion of America: Indians, Colonialism, and the Cant of Conquest*: 333, University of North Carolina Press, Chapel Hill
[6] Williamson, James A. ed. 1962; *The Cabot Voyages and Bristol Discovery under Henry VII*, Hakluyt Society Publications 2nd series CXX: 53
[7] Lewis, Bernard, 2003, *The Crisis of Islam: Holy War and Unholy Terror*: 55, The Modern Library, New York
[8] Canny, Nicolas, 1973, *The Ideology of English Colonization From Ireland to America*: 5
[9] 1673, Preface; *The Book of the General Laws for the People within the Jurisdiction of Connecticut*
[10] cited in Weinberg, Albert 1935, *Manifest Destiny, A Study of Nationalist Expansionism in American History*: 74-75
[11] Cotton, John, 1636, "The Bloudy Tenent, Washed and Made White in the Bloud of the Lambe" cited in Vaughan, Alden 1979, *New England Frontier: Puritans and Indians 1620-1675*: 119, Norton Press, New York
[12] 21 US 543: 576-577 (1823)
[13] Prucha, Francis, 1984, *The Great Father* v.1: 15-16, University of Nebraska Press, Lincoln
[14] Debates and Proceedings in the Congress of the United States, 4th Congress, 1st Session (1796): 893-895
[15] Colonial Records of Massachusetts, v.1: 170-171
[16] Cited in Andrews, Charles 1936, *The Colonial Period in American History*,: V.II: 78, Yale University Press, New Haven

[17] ibid1936: 107
[18] See Map #1 in Appendix A.
[19] See Pelletreau W. ed. 1910 *Southampton Town Records*, vol.5: 1-6 "Commission to James Farrett." A copy is also in the Connecticut State Archives, Towns and Lands, vol.1: no.6 (Letter of Agency) --- Alexander had originally received a grant from King Charles I in 1621 for the lands of Nova Scotia between the St Croix and St. Lawrence Rivers in Canada. In 1632, Charles I, in a treaty with France, agreed to return this land to French sovereignty. The King, in compensating Alexander for his loss, had him appointed to the Council of New England on January 29, 1635. Five days later he received a grant from the Council which included the island of "Mattowacks" (Long Island). Alexander died in February 1640. His oldest son Alexander, had died two years previous. Alexander's next surviving male heir, an infant grandson died within months of the Alexander's death. Under the English feudal concept of land tenure law (*primer seisin:* possession of the land by the crown upon the death of a royal grantee) if a grant holder died without heirs or committed a felony, the grant escheated to the King. Lord Claredon, the King's Chancellor, held the title on the Crowns behalf until the land was granted to the Kings brother, James the Duke of York in March of 1664. For a full rendering of Alexander and his Long Island grant see: Rife, Clarence W., 1931 The Earl of Stirling and the Colonization of Long Island in Essay's in Colonial History Presented to Charles McLean Andrews by his Students, 1931, New Haven, Yale University Press. See also, Stevens, John A. 1884, The English in New York 1664-1689 in Winsor J., ed. 1884 Narrative and Critical History of America Volume III. For the concept of *primer seisin* see: Harris, Marshall, 1953, Origin of the Land Tenure System in the United States: 24-27, Ames, Iowa State College Press.
[20] See Map #2 in Appendix A.
[21] O'Callahan, Edmund, ed, 1861, *Documents Relating to the Colonial History of New York*, vol. XIV: 29-31, Weed Parsons, New York
[22] Howell, G., 1866, *The Early History of Southampton L.I. New York*: 14-17; Adams, J., 1918, History of the Town of Southampton East of Canoe Place: 44-47
[23] cited in Adams 1918: 45
[24] Minutes of the Board of Trustees of the Freeholders and Commonalty of the Town of Southampton, Book 1: 50-51
[25] Minutes of the Board of Trustees of the Freeholders and Commonalty of the Town of Southampton Book 1: 45
[26] Minutes of the Board of Trustees of the Freeholders and Commonalty of the Town of Southampton Book 1: 49-50

[27] The Dutch States General laid claim to Long Island by virtue of Henrick (Henry) Hudson's September 1609 discovery of the Hudson River estuary. They also cited Adrian Block's 1614 exploration of Long Island Sound as further justification of their claims. New Netherland was established as a settlement by the Dutch West India Company by virtue of a charter from the States General in 1623. Cabot's 1496 chartered discovery of Long Island Sound preceded Hudson by 113 years.
[28] Minutes of the Board of Trustees of the Freeholders and Commonalty of the Town of Southampton Book 1: 47-48
[29] Records of the Town of Southampton, Book 1: 31
[30] Connecticut Colonial Records v.1: 566
[31] ibid: 567
[32] Pulsifer, D., 1859, *Acts of the Commissioners of the United Colonies of New England*, v.1: 21, William White Press, Boston
[33] Connecticut Colonial Records, v.1: 572
[34] Connecticut Colonial Records, v.2: 10
[35] Connecticut Colonial Records, v.1: 426-427

Chapter II

[1] Town of Southampton, Indian Papers 1640-1670: 2, "The first Agreement with Indians in Respect to Their Right to Plant Corn," December 28, 1649.
[2] Tooker, William W., 1911, *The Indian Place-Names On Long Island and Islands Adjacent*: 242, G. Putnam & Sons, New York
[3] It should also be noted that the Indians of central Long Island, such as the Unkechaug had a linguistic affinity with those Indian groups who occupied western Connecticut, especially along the Housatonic River Valley north into Massachusetts and west to the Mahican tribes in western New York State. Those Indian groups occupying western Long Island had a similar linguistic affinity with the Munsee Delaware Indians who occupied portions of the lower Hudson River valley, southern New Jersey and eastern Pennsylvania.
[4] Orr, Charles, 1884, *History of the Pequot War: The Contemporary Accounts of Mason, Underhill, Vincent And Gardner*, 137-138,: 144
[5] "eastern Long Island," Tooker, 1911: 182
[6] Records of the Colony of Plymouth Massachusetts, Volume IX: 18
[7] Stone, Gaynell S. ed., 1980, "Language and Lore of the Long Island Indians": 227, *Readings in Long Island Archaeology and Ethnohistory*, Vol. IV., Suffolk County Archaeology Association
[8] Records, Town of Southampton, Book B: 46, Deed from Wiandance to John Ogden, May 12, 1659.

[9] See in particular volume I of the Records of the Town of East-Hampton (1887, John Hunt, Sag Harbor): 179, the indenture of August 6, 1660 "btwne the ould Sachems Squa late wife of waindance disceased and her sonn Wianncombone...,": 198 " The old Suncks squa being enquired into the age of her sonn what age he was when he died..." (1662),: 199 "I the Suncks Squa with my sonne Waincombone did ye last yeare..."(1662).

[10] Pelletreau, William, 1874, *The First Book of Records of the Town of Southampton*: 1639-1660: 51(Deed of April 22,1648)

[11] ibid. 1874: 14-15

[12] Southampton Town Records,V.II: 176-180 (August 16, 1703)

[13] 1874,Pelletreau,W. *The First Book of Records of the Town of Southampton*: 1639-1660: 158.

[14] Philbrick, Nathaniel, 2006, *Mayflower: Story of Courage, Community, and War*: 209, New York Viking Press.

[15] For Pequot land cessions resulting from conquest see the Treaty of Hartford, September 21, 1638 in Vaughan, A, 1979, *New England Frontier*: 340-341. The loss of Pequannock lands via conquest can be found in Stratford (Connecticut) Land Records, vol.1: 243-244, Testimony of Thomas Stanton May 4, 1659 and in the Connecticut Colonial Records vol. 2: 339-340.

[16] Trumbull Benjamin. 1797, *A Complete History of Connecticut*, v.1: 99

[17] Connecticut Colonial Records, v.1: 2141650, Resolve of the General Court

[18] Acts & Laws of the Colony of Connecticut, 1661: 417 items 4, 5, 6, 7

[19] Connecticut Colonial Records, v.1: 552

[20] Acts & Laws of the Colony of Connecticut, 1702 ed.: 64

[21] Connecticut Colonial Records.v.1: 402

[22] The Dutch States General laid claim to Long Island by virtue of Henrick (Henry) Hudson's September 1609 discovery of the Hudson River estuary. They also cited Adrian Block's 1614 exploration of Long Island Sound as further justification of their claims. New Netherland was established as a settlement by the Dutch West India Company by virtue of a charter from the States General in 1623. John Cabot's 1496 chartered discovery of Long Island Sound preceded Hudson by 113 years.

[23] Book 1 Minutes of the Board of Trustees of the Freeholders and Commonalty of the Town of Southampton: 51

[24] Records of the Town of Southampton, volume 1: 162

Chapter III

[1] 1874, *The First Book of Records of the Town of Southampton*: 26, Sag Harbor, John H. Hunt.
[2] Southampton Town Records, Indian Papers 1640-1670 (transcribed): 2
[3] New York State Archives, Deed Book 2: 112, Agreement between the Indians and the Town of Southampton.
[4] The term "planting" used in colonial-era documents during the 17th and 18th century did not necessarily denote agricultural usage. Instead, its use was synonymous with the words "to settle," or "settling."
[5] Adams, James T., 1918, *History of the Town of Southampton (East of Canore Place)*79, Bridgehampton, Hampton Press.
[6] Pulsifer, David, 1859, *Records of the Colony of New Plymouth in New England, Acts of the Commissioners of the United Colonies of New England*, Vol. II 1653-1679: 98, Boston, William White.
[7] 1874, *The First Book of Records of the Town of Southampton*: 77-78, Sag Harbor, John H. Hunt.
[8] Connecticut Colonial Records, Vol. 1: 295, Order of the Connecticut General Court of Elections: Orders and Instructions to Capt John Mason; Indians near Southampton
[9] ibid. vol. 1: 532-533.

Chapter IV

[1] 1874, *The First Book of Records of the Town of Southampton*: 162, Sag Harbor, John H. Hunt
[2] 1874, *The First Book of Records of the Town of Southampton*: 176, Sag Harbor, John H. Hunt
[3] 1874, *The First Book of Records of the Town of Southampton*: 171, Sag Harbor, John H. Hunt/ Misc. Documents of the Town of Southampton 1649-1697#4
[4] 1874,*The First Book of Records of the Town of Southampton*, Volume 1: 166-168, Sag Harbor, John H. Hunt
[5] Pulsifer, David, 1859, *Records of Plymouth Colony Acts of the Commissioners of the United Colonies of New England*, Vol. II 1653-1678: 251, Boston William White.
[6] Connecticut Colonial Records, Vol.1: 365.
[7] Records of the Town of Southampton, volume 1: 167-168
[8] See in particular volume I of the *Records of the Town of East-Hampton* (1887, John Hunt, Sag Harbor): 179, the indenture of August 6, 1660 "btwne the ould Sachems Squa late wife of waindance disceased and her

sonn Wianncombone...,": 198 "The old Suncks squa being enquired into the age of her sonn what age he was when he died..." (1662),: 199 "I the Suncks Squa with my sonne Waincombone did ye last yeare..."(1662).

[9] Harrington, M.R., 1924, "An Ancient Village Site of the Shinnecock Indians," Anthropological Papers of the Museum of Natural History, Vo. XXII, Part V: 233.

[10] In 1661 John Winthrop Jr., the Governor of Connecticut was in England to petition the King for the Connecticut Colony Patent. While composing his petition to the King Winthrop emphasized that Long Island was to be included in the Patent. (Dunn, Richard, 1962, Puritans and Yankees: The Winthrop Dynasty of New England 1630-1717: 133)

[11] "...that no person in this Colony shall buy, hire, or receive as a gift any parcel of land or lands of any Indian or Indians, for the future except he does buy or receive the same for the use of the Colony or the benefit of some Town with the allowance of the court."

[12] An excellent commentary on the Duke of York, Nicolls and the political situation in the region can be found in Dunn, Richard, 1962, Puritans and Yankees: The Winthrop Dynasty of New England 1630-1747: 148-156. Having seized the Dutch Province by force, Nicolls received the Dutch surrender at Fort Amsterdam (the present-day Battery on lower Manhattan Island, which Nicolls renamed Fort James). In the 1668 Treaty of Breda, formally ending the conflict between England and the Dutch States, the Dutch confirmed the English to be in rightful possession of New Netherland. Nicolls governed the province under the Dukes Patent until the advent of the Third Anglo-Dutch War (1672-1674). In August of 1673 Dutch forces seized New York from the English. Under the conditions for the cessation of hostilities stipulated in the February 1674 Treaty of Westminster the Dutch returned possession of New York to the King. When the Dutch conquered the Province, the Duke of York's Provincial grant ceased to be effective by 'right of conquest'. Connecticut quickly tried to take advantage of this 'void' by reasserting her claim under Charles II 1662 Charter, to Eastern Long Island. The Duke's brother King Charles II quickly had his brother's grant reconfirmed on June 29, 1674. Nicolls was allowed to return to England. He was replaced as Provincial Governor by Sir Edmund Andros.

[13] Book 1 Minutes of the Board of Trustees of the Freeholders and Commonalty of the Town of Southampton: 54;Town of Southampton, Historical Documents 1637-1869: 74A-74B

[14] New York State Archives, Deed Book 2: 257, November 6,1667.

[15] New York State Archives, Deed Book 2: 200-201, March 13, 1666.

[16] The First Book of Indian Records of the Town of Southampton: 169

[17] This was the last document in the historical record within which Weany Sunk participated. It is surmised she died shortly thereafter. Her passing may have been the trigger that caused the political fissioning amongst the Shinnecock.
[18] The First Book of Records of the Town of Southampton: 1639-1660: 169
[19] Paltsits, V.H, 1910, *Minutes of the Executive Council of the Province of New York*: Administration of Francis Lovelace, vol.II: 684-685.

Chapter V

[1] Minutes of the Executive Council of the Province of New York 1668-1673, Vol. II. No. XXIX.
[2] O'Callahan, E.B., 1859, *Documents Relating to the Colonial History of the State of New York*, vol. XIV: 647, Albany Weed Parsons
[3] The Second Book of Records of the Town of Southampton Long Island, New York: 202-203.
[4] The First Book of Records of the Town of Southampton: 14-15

Chapter VI

[1] O'Callahan, E. B. Fenrow, W. 1862, *Documentary History of New York*, Vol.1: 665, Albany Weed Parsons. "A List of ye Inhabitants of ye Towne of Southampton, old and young, Christians and Hethen ffremen and servants, white and black Anno 1698"
[2] Southampton Town Records,V.II: 176-180
[3] Southampton Town Records,Vol.II: 358-359.
[4] See Map #4 I Appendix A.
[5] Book 1, Minutes of the Board of trustees of the Freeholders and Commonalty of the Town of Southampton: 57-58

Chapter VII

[1] "First Journal of Mr. Azariah Horton, October 17, 1742, to March 5, 1743," in 1993, *The History and Archaeology of the Montauk*: 213, Suffolk County Archaeological Society.
[2] An examination of the citations provided by the Shinnecock in: Sleight H. 1931, Trustees Records: Southampton, New York, Part Two 1741-1826, depicting such Town-Tribal interactions reveals that the actions of the

Southampton Town Trustees were unilateral with no tribal presence or input at these meetings until after 1790.

[3] Sleight, Henry D. ed. Trustees Records: Southampton, New York 1741-1826,: 255-257

[4] The Third Book of Records of the Town of Southampton Long Island, New York: 78-79; Southampton Records1731-1809: 153

[5] Sleight, Harry, D. ed. Trustees Records: Southampton, New York 1741-1826 Part 1: 150

[6] The Third Book of Records of the Town of Southampton Long Island, New York: 146-147

[7] Sleight, Harry D. ed., Trustees Records: Southampton, New York 1741-1826 Part 1: 174-175

[8] Sleight, Harry D. ed., Trustees Records: Southampton, New York 1741-1826 Part 1: 428

[9] ibid: 150,: 155,: 196,: 291,: 334

[10] Woodward, 1995, *East Hampton: A Town and Its People 1648-1994*: 124. Indeed, as early as 1713 the Town of East Hampton was noting "the scarcity of timber at Montauk." (Records, Town of East Hampton, vol.III: 300) One hundred years later, the Gazetteer of New York (1813, Horatio Spofford ed.: 301-302) reported "Southampton sends large quantities of cordwood to New York [City]" a situation that undoubtedly contributed to the rapid deforestation of the area.

[11] Dwight, Timothy,1823 ed. *Travels in New England and New York, Journey to Long Island, Letter III*

[12] Sleight, Harry, D. ed., Trustees Records: Southampton, New York 1741-1826, pt.1: 6

[13] Sleight, Henry D. ed. Trustees Records: Southampton, New York 1741-1826,: 34

[14] ibid: 44

[15] ibid: 26

[16] ibid Sleight: 57-58

[17] Sleight, Harry, D. ed., Trustees Records: Southampton, New York 1741-1826: 488-489

[18] ibid: 489

[19] Southampton Indian Papers 1680-1806

[20] Sleight, Harry D, ed, Trustees Records: Southampton, New York 1741-1826: 384-385

[21] Geertz, Clifford, 1979, *The Interpretation of Cultures*: 99, New York Basic Books

[22] Eells, Earnst, mss. "Indian Missions on Long Island," East Hampton Library.

[23] "First Journal of Mr. Azariah Horton August 5th 1741, to November 1st 1741," in, Stone, Gaynell ed., 1993, *The History and Archaeology of the Montauk Indians*: 197, Suffolk County Archaeological Association, 2nd edition.
[24] Sleight, Harry D, ed., Trustees Records: Southampton, New York 1741-1826: 514
[25] Annual Report of the Board of Directors to the New York Missionary Society: 8-9: 17, New York, George Forman.
[26] Prime, Nathanel S., 1845, *History of Long Island from its First Settlement by Europeans to the Year 1845*: 115, New York, Robert Carter.
[27] Eells, Earnest, E.,1939, "Indian Missions on Long Island": 170, in *Journal of the Department of History of the Presbyterian Church*, Vol. XVIII, No. 7.
[28] in the Canoe Place Division, Lot #18, between the Riverhead Road and the Quag Road (Montauk Highway).
[29] Ales, Marian F., 1979, "A History of the Indians on Montauk, Long Island," in *The History and Archaeology of the Montauk Indians*: 115, Suffolk County Archaeological Association
[30] Prine Nathanel S., 1845, *History of Long Island from its First Settlement by Europeans to the Year 1845*: 217, New York, Robert Carter.
[31] Southampton Town Records, vol. III: 123-132.
[32] Southampton Town Records, vol. VI: 252.
[33] The Sixth Volume of Record Of Southampton, Abstracts of Vol.II Deeds: 254.
[34] Last Will and Testament of Moses Culver, June 22, 1837, Sufflok County Records, Unacknowledged Deeds, Liber 2: 301-302.
[35] Prime Nathanel S., 1845, *History of Long Island from its First Settlement by Europeans to the Year 1845*: 217, New York, Robert Carter.
[36] Downs, James Y., 1887, "History of Shinnecock 1662-1887": 19-20, unpublished mss. Penneypacker Library, Long Island Collection, East Hampton, New York.
[37] Prime, 1845: 216.
[38] Downs, c.1887: 20.
[39] Prime, 1845: Appendix 1, 217.
[40] Prime, 1845: 217.
[41] Downs, c.1887: 20
[42] Prime, 1845: 217.
[43] ibid: 5.
[44] Indian Records, 1793-1833, Town of Southampton, April 16, 1796
[45] Indian Records, 1793-1833, Town of Southampton, April 6, 1813
[46] Indian Records, 1793-1833, Town of Southampton, April 8, 1816

[47] Downs, James Y.,1887, History of Shinnecock 1662-1887: 19-20, unpublished mss. Penneypacker Library, Long Island Collection, East Hampton, New York.
[48] Trustee Records of the Town of Southampton N.Y., Part Two, 1741-1826: 309
[49] The Fourth Book of Records, Town of Southampton 1807-1873.
[50] Trustee Records of the Town of Southampton N.Y., Part Two, 1741-1826: 310

Chapter VIII

[1] Trustee Records of the Town of Southampton, N.Y 1741-1826, Part 1: 384
[2] Trustee Records of the Town of Southampton, N.Y 1741-1826: 488-489
[3] Trustee Records of the Town of Southampton, N.Y 1741-1826: 514
[4] State of New York, Index to Senate Journals,1777-1799: 15, January 24, 1792.
[5] An Act for the Benefit of the Shinnecock Tribe of Indians, residing in Suffolk county.15th Session Chapter 15.Laws of the State of New York, vol.3: 280-281
[6] Southampton Indian Records 1793-1833
[7] Town of Southampton, Indian Records Book 1, April 3, 1792-May 3,1792: 4
[8] Trustee Records of the Town of Southampton, N.Y 1741-1826 part 1: 541.
[9] ibid: 552
[10] Indian Records Book 2, Town of Southampton: 1793-1833: 2
[11] Indian Records Book 2, Town of Southampton: 1793-1833: 10-11
[12] Southampton Indian Records 1793-1833
[13] Southampton Indian Records 1793-1833
[14] ibid: 33
[15] Laws of New York, Chap 147: 373. Shinnecock Indians Special Provisions Concerning.
[16] Trustee Records of the Town of Southampton Part 2, 1741-1826: 249-250
[17] Indian Records Book 2, Town of Southampton: 1793-1833: 39
[18] Trustee Records of the Town of Southampton 1741-1826: 138-139
[19] Trustees Records of the Town of Southampton 1741-1826: 141
[20] Southampton Indian Papers: 1640-1806; Opinion of Indian lease terms.
[21] Trustees Records of the Town of Southampton 1741-1826: 219
[22] Indian Records Book 2, Town of Southampton: 1793-1833: 42

[23] Trustee Records of the Town of Southampton 1741-1826, Part 1: 57-58
[24] Indian Records, Town of Southampton, 1793-1833
[25] Laws of New York Chapter CXXIII: 150-151; An Act relating to the Shinnecock tribe of Indians.
[26] Trustee Records of the Town of Southampton 1741-1826, Part 2: 249-250,: 270,: 273
[27] Trustee Records of the Town of Southampton 1741-1826, Part 2: 249-250 (May 13, 1818)
[28] New York Assembly Papers, Vol. 41 1809-1832, New York State Archives
[29] Southampton Indian Papers: 1640-1806; Opinion of Indian lease terms.
[30] Trustee Records of the Town of Southampton 1741-1826, Part 2: 141
[31] Trustee Records of the Town of Southampton 1741-1826, Part 2: 278
[32] 1861, *Gazetteer of the State of New York* tenth edition: 638, Southampton.
[33] ibid: 638
[34] Prime, Nathanel, 1845, *History of Long Island, from its First Settlement by Europeans to the Year 1845*: 101, Robert Carter, New York
[35] Trustee Records of the Town of Southampton 1741-1826, Part 2: 297
[36] Town of Southampton, Trustee Meeting Minutes, June 27, 1837
[37] Town of Southampton, Trustee Meeting Minutes,, April 1,1848
[38] Trustee Records of the Town of Southampton 1741-1826, Part 2: 308-309
[39] Town of Southampton, Trustee Meeting Minutes, April 11, 1843
[40] grass and /or rush covered lands.
[41] Town of Southampton, Trustee Meeting Minutes, April 13, 1849
[42] Suffolk County Action File #502, New York Supreme Court, Suffolk County, Austin Rose v. Luther Bun et al.

Chapter IX

[1] Prime, Nathaniel S. 1845, *History of Long Island, from its First Settlement by Europeans to the Year 1845*. Robert Carter, New York.
[2] French, J. H., 1861, *Gazetteer of the State of New York* tenth edition: 638, Southampton.
[3] Trustee Records of the Town of Southampton 1741-1826, Part 2: 308-309
[4] Meeting Records of the Proprietors of the Town of Southampton 1855: 53
[5] Meeting Records of the Proprietors of the Town of Southampton 1858: 55b-56

[6] Manuscript Division, New York State Archives, Albany, "Petition of the Trustees of the Proprietors of the Common and Undivided Lands in the town of Southampton, January 7, 1859"

[7] Luther Bunn, James Bun, and David Bunn bought a complaint action against the Town Trustees that was filed on July 26, 1859 with the Suffolk County Supreme Court in an attempt to nullify both the State enactment and the subsequent land exchange by arguing that a 1,000 year lease was the legal equivalent to a conveyance in fee by the Town of the former lease lands. The Court rejected their complaint.

[8] March 16, 1859, An Act to enable the Shinnecock Tribe of Indians to exchange certain rights in land with the Trustees of the Proprietors of the Common & Undivided Lands & Marshes in the Town of Southampton. Laws of the State of New York, 82nd Session of the Legislature Albany: 101-103 Chap. 46

[9] Suffolk County Records, Liber 103: 257

[10] See Map #3 in Appendix A.

[11] Meeting Records of the Proprietors of the Town of Southampton, 1861: 59

Chapter X

[1] Bernstein, David, 2003, "A Stage 1 Archaeological Survey for the Shinnecock Reservation-West Hills Hampton Bays, Town of Southampton Suffolk County New York," Institute for Long Island Archaeology, Stony Brook, New York

[2] see Harris, Marshall, 1953, Origin of the Land Tenure System in the United States, Ames, Iowa State College Press; Bushman, Richard, 1967, From Puritan to Yankee: Character and the Social Order in Connecticut, 1690-1765, Cambridge, Harvard University Press; The Second and Third volumes, Book of Records of the Town of Southampton Long Island, N.Y. 1877, Sag Harbor, John B. Hunt; Sleight, Henry ed. 1931, Trustees Records of the Town of Southampton N.Y., Parts I. and II. 1741-1826, Sag Harbor.

[3] Southampton Town Records v.III: 123-128

[4] Southampton Town Records v.III: 129-132

[5] Southampton Historical Society, W. K. Dunwell Papers, Folder 7

[6] See Map #5 in Appendix A.

[7] Suffolk County Records, Suffolk Court, Court Actions, File 598: 117

[8] 1888, Report of Special Committee to Investigate the Indian Problem in the State of New York.: 830

[9] See Map #6 in Appendix A.

[10] ibid.1888: 851
[11] Records of the Indian Trustees, April 7, 1808
[12] Hodge F. 1906, *Handbook of American Indians* Part 1: 812-813, Part 2: 550-551, Bureau of American Ethnology Bulletin 30, Washington D.C. Smithsonian Institute
[13] Southampton Town Records v.III: 123-128
[14] Suffolk County Records, Liber Deed 191: 403
[15] Suffolk County Justice Records, Carpenter Case, Documents 32-32d
[16] Record Book of Trustees of tribe of Shinnecock Indians 1909-1926: 363
[17] Southampton Town-Indian Records 1880-1908: 20
[18] ibid: 24
[19] ibid: 25
[20] ibid: 30
[21] ibid: 32
[22] Suffolk County Records, Liber 191: 403-404
[23] Southampton Town Records, Vol. III: 123-132
[24] Suffolk County Records, Assistant Clerk Mortgage Liber D: 17-18 1801; Assistant Clerk Mortgage Liber H: 358-359,1824; Assistant Clerk Mortgage Liber J: 54; Unacknowledged Deeds Liber 2; Moses and Phoebe Culver to Eliza White,1804 (abutted on North by Beach, east Israel Conklin
[25] Suffolk County Deeds, Liber J: 9-10, 1824; Liber 46: 316-317, 1847; Liber U: 190-191: 120 1834;Liber 42: 153,1845
[26] Suffolk County Records, Liber 46: 316-317, 1847
[27] Suffolk County Records, Liber 95: 536, 1857
[28] Supreme Court, Suffolk County, Finding 2/23/22, Shinnecock Tribe v Hubbard
[29] Suffolk County Records, Liber 554: 19, 1904
[30] Suffolk County Records, Liber 845: 380-381
[31] Suffolk County Records, Liber 699: 48, 1909
[32] Suffolk County Records, Liber 305: 306, 1858
[33] Suffolk County Records Liber 191: 403,1873
[34] C.M. Raynor Survey of April 8,1963
[35] Lewis, Bernard, 1972, *History: Remembered, Recovered, Invented*: 58-59, Princeton, Princeton University Press

Appendix

Maps

*All maps, with the exception of the
Town of Southampton 2004 Map (issued by the Town's EIS Department),
are from the Map Files, Special Collections Room,
State University of New York at Stonybrook Library.*

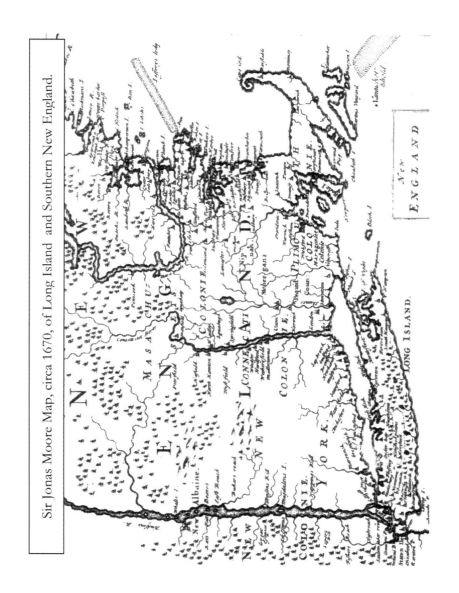

Sir Jonas Moore Map, circa 1670, of Long Island and Southern New England.

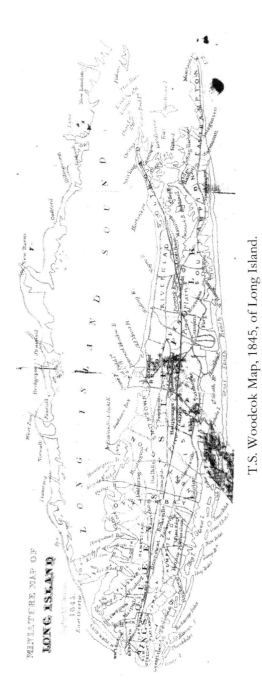

T.S. Woodcok Map, 1845, of Long Island.

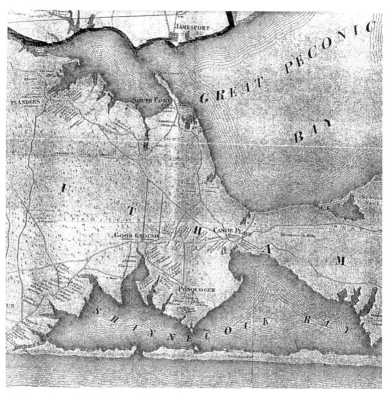

Map, circa 1870, Central Southampton depicting the location of Shinnecock Neck (Shinnecock Indians), Shinnecock Hills, Sebonac Neck, and Canoe Place.

(continued from page 160)

U.S. Geological Survey Map, 1797, depicting (in the darkened area) the 1703 Indian lease region, the location of the "Indian Meeting House at Sebonas/Coldsprings, Shinnecock Great Neck, and Canoe Place."

(continued from page 162)

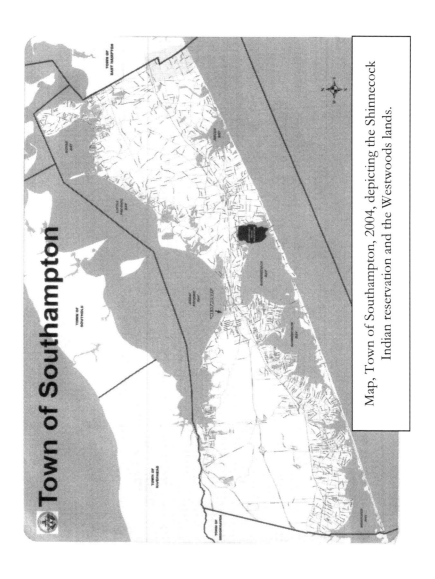

Map, Town of Southampton, 2004, depicting the Shinnecock Indian reservation and the Westwoods lands.

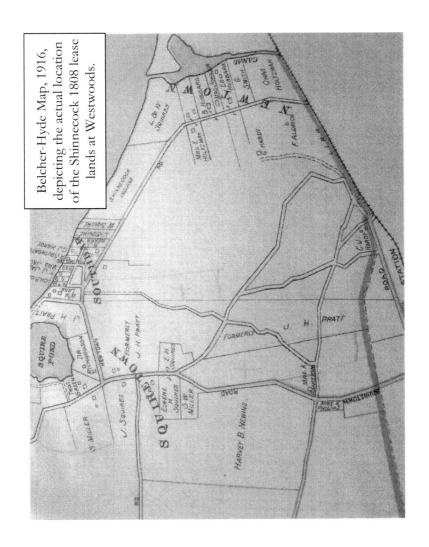

Belcher-Hyde Map, 1916, depicting the actual location of the Shinnecock 1808 lease lands at Westwoods.

About the Author

Mr. James P. Lynch is a nationally recognized Ethno-historical research consultant. He has authored numerous books, research publications, and articles on tribal land claims, tribal sovereignty, tribal recognition, historical land title, tribal land into trust issues, and tribal history. His professional services are used by law firms, local, state and federal officials and agencies, and private sectors such as businesses, authors and network news media. He has also testified as a qualified expert witness on historical and anthropological issues in federal and state courts. Mr. Lynch is the owner of Connecticut-based Historical Consulting and Research Services LLC. He can be contacted at jajpl@aol.com.

Made in the USA
Middletown, DE
03 February 2020